A Teacher's Guide to Classroom Research

David Hopkins

OPEN UNIVERSITY PRESS

Milton Keynes . Philadelphia

Open University Press
12 Cofferidge Close
Stony Stratford
Milton Keynes MK11 1BY England
and
242 Cherry Street
Philadelphia PA 19106 USA

First Published 1985

Reprinted 1987, 1988 , 1989

Copyright © David Hopkins 1985

British Library Cataloguing in Publication Data

Hopkins, David
    A teacher's guide to classroom research.
    1. Education—Research   2. Teaching
    I. Title
    371.1'02'072   LB1028

ISBN 0-335-15028-4

Library of Congress Cataloging in Publication Data

Hopkins, David.
    A teachers guide to classroom research.

    Bibliography: p.
    Includes index.
    1. Education—Research.   2. Classroom management—
Research.   3. Observation (Educational method)
4. Curriculum change,   I. Title.
LB1028.H586 1985   370'.7'8   84-27178

ISBN 0-335-15028-4 (pbk.)

Typeset by Mathematical Composition Setters
Salisbury, UK
Printed in Great Britain by St Edmundsbury Press Ltd
Bury St Edmunds, Suffolk

To those who have helped me move
towards the ideas expressed here:
my parents, students, and colleagues
in the invisible college, especially
GE, MFW, DBC, MG, LAS and JR.

In short the outstanding characteristics of the extended professional (teacher) is a capacity for autonomous professional self development through systematic self study, through the study of the work of other teachers and through the testing of ideas by classroom research procedures.

Lawrence Stenhouse – *An Introduction to Curriculum Research and Development*

Appreciating a phenomenon is a fateful decision, for it eventually entails a commitment – to the phenomenon and to those exemplifying it – to render it with fidelity and without violating its integrity. Entering the world of the phenomenon is a radical and drastic method of appreciation.

David Matza – *Becoming Deviant*

Contents

Acknowledgements

I am grateful to Mike Bruce, Don Cochrane, Peter Norman, Jean Rudduck and especially Ann Kilcher for the care with which they reviewed the manuscript; and for conversations that clarified my thinking on this and other matters. Their friendship and professional collaboration have meant a great deal to me. Although they may not agree with everything in this book, or with the way in which I have tackled the issues, their contributions have immeasurably improved what is here.

Suzzane de Castell, Gill Harper–Jones, Pat Holborn, my sister Mary Hopkins, Louise Pelletier and David Pritchard also provided material and intellectual support at critical and opportune times: my thanks to them too.

A number of colleagues and students have graciously allowed me to use some of their material as illustrations and examples in the book. In this regard I am indebted to Stan Auerbach, Judy Byer, Heather Lockhart, Sandra Meister, Marianne Schmidt, Ann Waldo and Harvey Walker.

John Skelton, my publisher at the Open University Press, has been most supportive throughout the enterprise; and the three anonymous reviewers for the book made comments that encouraged me to revise and improve the manuscript. I anticipate that at least two of them will be satisfied with the outcome.

The argument of the book was developed from ideas originally presented in papers published in the *CARN Bulletin*, *Phi Delta Kappan*, and *School Organisation*. Finally, I must acknowledge the Deakin University Press, Universitetsforlaget AS and particularly John Elliott and the Ford Teaching Project for allowing me to reproduce copyright material.

1

Introduction: A Teacher's Guide to Classroom Research

This is a practical guide for teachers who wish to undertake research in their classrooms and schools for the purpose of improving practice. Classroom research, in the sense that I refer to it here, is an act undertaken by teachers either to improve their own or a colleague's teaching or to test the assumptions of educational theory in practice. Classroom research generates hypotheses about teaching from the experience of teaching, and encourages teachers to use this research to make their teaching more competent. So when I write of classroom research or of the teacher as researcher, I am not envisioning scores of teachers assuming a research role and carrying out research projects to the exclusion of their teaching. My vision is of teachers who have extended their role to include critical reflection upon their craft with the aim of improving it.

Although lip service is often paid to this idea, we live in an educational system and society that tends to limit individual initiative and responsibility and encourage conformity and control. Teachers and pupils (and society too) deserve better than that. Undertaking research in their own classrooms is one way in which teachers can take increased responsibility for their actions and create a more energetic and dynamic environment in which teaching and learning can occur

The origins of teacher research as a movement can be traced back to the Humanities Curriculum Project (HCP) with its emphasis on an experimental curriculum and the reconceptualization of curriculum development as curriculum research. HCP, in its attempt to encourage a non-partisan and critically reflective attitude to teaching on the part of teachers, had a radical and controversial influence on teaching in British schools during the 1970s.

Following HCP, the concept of teacher research was nurtured by John Elliott and Clem Adelman in the Ford Teaching Project. The project involved 40 primary, intermediate and high school teachers who aspired to enquiry/ discovery methods of teaching in examining their classroom practice through action research. These teachers developed hypotheses about their teaching which could be shared with other teachers and used to enhance their own teaching. The Ford Teaching Project published many teacher-researcher case studies and booklets on research techniques, and also organized research conferences solely for teachers. This gave an enormous boost to the teacher–researcher movement.

At about the same time, Lawrence Stenhouse, who directed the Humanities Curriculum Project, further popularized the concept of 'the teacher as researcher' by utilizing it as the major theme in his influential book, *An Introduction to Curriculum Research and Development*. Encouraged by the considerable impact that Stenhouse had on the theory and practice of curriculum and teaching, and the popularity and publicity enjoyed by the Ford Teaching Project, the teacher research movement has mushroomed. As well as burgeoning teacher research groups in the U.K., Australia, the U.S. and Canada, there are pockets of teacher–researchers in Scandinavia, France, Chile and elsewhere. Although teacher research was not an entirely new concept in the late sixties, it is from this period that it became an identifiable movement.

All books emerge out of a specific set of individual circumstances that have influenced the author, and this book is no exception. The journey that preceded this book is still continuing, and so the story is and will continue to be unfinished. But two staging posts have been crucial in developing the ideas presented here and provide a context in which to consider the book.

The first influence is the work of Lawrence Stenhouse. In the Humanities Curriculum Project and his other work, Stenhouse was primarily concerned with emancipation. The creation of individual meaning in a non-authoritarian context is a central aspect of his concept of emancipation. HCP utilized a teaching strategy designed to emancipate the individual pupil from the control of authoritative knowledge. There were three aspects to the HCP teaching strategy: the place of discussion, the use of documents as evidence to inform discussion, and the assumption of the role of the teacher as neutral chairperson. By adopting this pedagogical format, Stenhouse was moving away from a teacher dominated classroom to a setting where pupils, unconstrained by the authority of the teacher, could create meaning for themselves on the basis of evidence and discussion.

If HCP was in part a curriculum designed to emancipate pupils, the phrase 'teacher as researcher' was intended to do the same for teachers. Teachers are too often the servants of heads, advisers, researchers, text books, curriculum developers, examination boards, or the Department of Education and Science among others. By adopting a research stance, teachers are liberating themselves from the control position they so often find themselves in. I should also add that Stenhouse utilized this approach in HCP, where he encouraged teachers to follow the specification of a curriculum but at the same time to assess it critically: to assume that the curriculum proposal was intelligent but not necessarily correct and to monitor its effectiveness in the classroom. By adopting this critical approach, by taking a research stance, the teacher is engaged not only in a meaningful professional development activity but also engaged in a process of refining, and becoming more autonomous in, professional judgement.

The second influence on this book is more personal. During the seventies, I trained as a teacher and taught, worked as an Outward Bound instructor and mountain guide, and read for postgraduate degrees in education. Although somewhat different activities, they were all characterized by a desire, often hesitant and naive, to create ways in which people could take more control of their own lives. Irrespective of the context – practice teaching, an 'O' level history class, counselling a 'delinquent' pupil, assisting in a youth club, on the rock face, out in the wilderness, or discussing ideas in a seminar – there were similarities in overall aim and pedagogic structure.

Later, as a teacher in a Canadian University, I taught courses in curriculum development, analysis of teaching, classroom research, and found in Stenhouse's work a theoretical framework within which I could put my ideas into action. This book has emerged from that experience, more specifically from a course I teach in classroom research and some papers I wrote on the topic (Hopkins 1982, 1984 a, b). Thus, the book is based on a set of ideas that have the enhancement of teacher judgement and autonomy as a specific goal, and is grounded within the practical realities of teachers and students.

The book has a modest aim: it is to provide teachers and students with a practical guide to doing research in their own classrooms. Most of the work on teacher research is either philosophical discussion (Rudduck and Hopkins, 1985), reports by researchers (Elliott and Adelman, 1976) or teacher's own accounts of their research (Nixon, 1981); little work exists on how to go about doing teacher based classroom research in a practical and straightforward way. In this sense the book complements the existing literature, rather than competing with it. As a guide for those who wish to undertake research in their own classrooms, I hope principally that practising and intending teachers will find the book useful. I also anticipate that teachers on inservice courses, advisers and education tutors will be able to use it profitably.

After this introduction, a few case studies of teacher based research are given to provide a context for what follows. In chapter three, two arguments are considered for teacher based research – the need for professionalism in teaching, and the inadequacy of the traditional research approach in helping teachers improve their teaching. In chapter four, action research, which has become the main vehicle for teacher research, is discussed and critiqued;

from that discussion five criteria for teacher based research are suggested. The following chapter discusses the ways in which teacher research problems are formulated and initiated. Chapters six and seven describe various ways of gathering information on and observing classroom behaviour. Chapter eight describes a method for analysing this data. These three chapters constitute the heart of the teacher research process. Chapter nine discusses ways in which classroom research can be reported, published, linked to the curriculum and utilized in school improvement strategies. In 'A Final Word', I stand back a little and discuss the relationship between classroom research and teacher professionalism.

2

Cases in Point

Often the phrase classroom research brings to mind images of researchers undertaking research in a sample of schools or classrooms and using as subjects the teachers and students who live out their educational lives within them. Often this image is correct. This book, however, is about another kind of research in which teachers look critically at their own classrooms primarily for the purpose of improving their teaching and the quality of life in their classrooms. Because the reader is less likely to be familiar with the latter type of research, it might be useful to begin with some examples of classroom research undertaken by teachers.

The first example is a case study by Sandra Meister, a first year teacher who was taking an inservice course.

The purpose of this research project is to become familiar with educational research within the classroom, to analyse and improve one aspect of my teaching style. But I have had some difficulty in pinpointing which aspect of my teaching I wished to focus on. As a harried first year teacher, I really had not given much time to actually thinking about the way I taught, rather I tended to worry about keeping things peaceful until the three o'clock bell rang. I decided, however, to look at the types of questions I asked, the order in which I asked them, and to whom the questions were directed. This sequence appears to be the key to training a child to think independently. In order to become more aware of my own teaching style, I decided to obtain data from myself as teacher, from my class, and from an outside observer who was previously unknown to myself and my students.

Social studies was an area I find particularly dull at this level. The entire primary curriculum centres around 'myself and my family in our community', 'components of our community', and finally 'the interaction of communities'. The lessons I had taught were rather scattered and poorly sequenced. As a final unit, I decided to divide the class into three groups and have one group research communities of the past, one look at Prince George as it is today, and one group design a community for the future. Most of the knowledge came from group lessons and discussions where, through various questions and brainstorming techniques, I hoped to direct the student to some logical conclusions as to the necessary requirements for community life.

The lesson used as the basis for the research was on different modes of communication. I taught the lesson while the observer recorded the types of questions asked (ie. fact, critical thinking, explanation, yes/no, etc.), which students responded and the teacher reaction to the response. The data was gathered by the observer using a checklist. The lesson was also audio-taped which enabled both the teacher and the observer to review the data afterwards.

The results were really quite an eye opener. The majority of my questions required critical thinking or an opinion while the remainder were questions for the purpose of gathering facts. Most of the questions required one or two word answers. The following is an analysis of my questioning techniques.

Types of questions asked: on the positive side, most of the questions required critical thinking, i.e. 'How would you feel ...?' 'What would you do if ...?' Many questions required students to express an opinion, I avoided Yes/No questions which is something I was pleased to note. On the negative side, I seemed to avoid asking any questions which required any type of explanation. This is an important area which I have overlooked.

Sequence of questions asked: the order in which the

questions were asked seemed logical and new information was built on previous answers. The weakest area here seemed to be in moving from one topic to the next. I'll need to work on having a few key questions as pivot points for my lesson.

To whom questions were directed: on the positive side, I would often ask one question such as, 'Who do you talk to on the phone?' and randomly choose many students for a one word answer which keeps them all involved and interested. On the negative side, whenever I asked an open question I seemed to respond to one of three students regardless of who may have had their hands up. These particular students are those with whom I try and avoid confrontations.

Teacher responses to answers: this is the area which I feel this project has identified as something for me to question. As I looked at the data, I realized that I rarely praised the students verbally. The majority of teacher responses were repeating what the child said and nodding to affirm their stance. The next frequent teacher response was no reaction. The observer noted that the students seemed satisfied with the way their opinions were accepted without much comment and did'nt appear to act differently when verbal praise was given. I also appeared to accept an answer regardless of whether hands were up or not.

There are three areas where the observer and I saw possibilities for improvement. The first is to accept answers and request answers from all students rather than a select few. An obvious way to improve this is to limit the size of the group to whom the lesson is being taught. Perhaps using a phrase such as 'let's let someone else have a turn' would help. The changes need not be large and I'm glad this was brought to my attention – imagine some poor child spending a year in my class and never being asked a question!

The second area for change is in making a smooth transition from one topic to the next within a lesson. I feel this can be accomplished by noting beforehand a comparison phrase or question and recording differences or similarities between the two topics.

Finally, I must learn to allow the children an opportunity to give detailed explanations. This is an ideal opportunity for improving verbal lucidity and compositional skills.

After some reflection on the research project, I feel that it was a valuable exercise. Having another individual working on the project immediately reduced the feelings of isolation I had from the staff.

The other area that was most valuable was the opportunity to go through a research project under guidance from an experienced researcher.

Now that contacts have been established, the feasibility of classroom research in Prince George has expanded. Having completed the process once makes a world of difference for considering future research projects.

The next time I conduct or participate in a research project, I will use the 'triangulation approach'. The insight of an outside observer is invaluable and also allows the students to offer some feedback. I would also like to participate in a project where the observer would be the director (adviser) and have more than one classroom involved. By playing a small role in a larger scale project, I feel I would gain more first-hand knowledge and become confident in being a teacher–researcher.

The second case study is by Ann Waldo, an experienced teacher who had previously been involved in a classroom research.

Bruce Joyce and Beverly Showers (1984) maintain that teachers when given adequate training conditions are consistently able to fine-tune existing skills and learn new ones. However, they point out that learning a new skill does not guarantee being able to transfer a skill vertically to higher order, more complex tasks. Early-task learning has been found to maximize transfer if the tasks are relevant to the acquisition of a teaching model.

My school district has been encouraging teachers to use cognitive models of teaching. Bloom's Taxonomy and the Renzuli Triad Model have specifically been suggested as the models to be used to provide an enriched curriculum. Last year, teachers had inservice training on these approaches and this included theory and demonstation with adults. The demonstration teams were young, enthusiastic and well-prepared fellow teachers. The teachers went back to their classrooms ready to implement higher order thinking. Despite using devices such as specific question words to elicit different levels of responses, most teachers found it very difficult to do this.

After watching a video tape of myself teaching and failing to allow students think-time before responding, I wondered if this inability in an early task could have caused some of the difficulties I experienced in using Bloom's Taxonomy and Renzuli's Triad Model, as both models are dependent on students' ability to articulate their thoughts. Verbalizing high level thinking demands that time is spent formulating the response. The other two primary teachers in my school had only moderate success in implementing the new models.

I decided that for this piece of research I would ask these teachers to consciously extend think-time to the recommended 3 to 5 seconds, I hypothesized that this would lead to lengthier student responses and higher order questions from the teacher. Hopefully, the teachers would also begin to internalize this early-task learning and be better equipped to implement other models of teaching that are dependent on student response.

The subjects were a Grade 1 teacher (S1) who has taught for 27 years and a Grade 2 teacher (S2) who has taught for 14 years. Both agreed to audio tape a session of directed reading to provide baseline data. They were informed that they would be asked to alter one aspect of their teaching which, in turn, was expected to cause a change to occur. It was decided that allowing the teachers to audio tape themselves would disturb students and teachers less than an observer or a video tape. S2 taped a group with low academic ability. S1 taped a group with average ability.

The baseline tapes were interpreted by myself. Think-time between each teacher question and response was recorded. If a response came less than 1 second after the question, it was designated 0 seconds. The number of words in each student response was counted. Each question was related to level 1, 2, 3, 4, 5 or 6 responses according to Bloom's Taxonomy. The hierarchy in Blooms's Taxonomy is: 1. knowledge, 2. comprehension, 3. application, 4. analysis, 5. synthesis, and 6. evaluation. As S1 had taped only 13 questions and resonses I decided to use the first 10 questions on each tape, provided they were not repetitions or rephrasings.

This data was discussed with the teachers on the following day except for the hierarchical rating of the questions. This was not mentioned. They were asked to read an excerpt from 'Extending Think-Time for Better Reading Instruction' by Linda Gambrell (1981). In this excerpt, the author stresses that the teacher must be prepared for leaden silences and resist the temptation to fill them. The student must also be prepared by the teacher to accept the think-time for thinking instead of unproductive hand waving in the belief that responding is a speed competition. Lastly, she stresses that it takes time for teachers and students to slow down. There was no mention of higher levels of questions or responses.

The teachers, therefore, were set to extend think-time in the hope of lengthening student responses. They were asked to tape themselves three more times with the same reading groups but it was explained that these tapes would be for self-monitoring rather than for data. They were encouraged to extend think-time whenever appropriate in the classroom in order to get more practice.

Six school days after the baseline data had been collected the teachers were again asked to tape their guided reading in order to provide data for the research. They were reminded to use the same reading groups as for the baseline data. The data from these tapes was used in exactly the same manner as the baseline tapes.

For both teachers there was an increase in the length of student response when think-time was increased as seen in Table 2.1. There was also a small increase in the hierarchical level of questions posed to the students by the teachers. These results cannot be said to be statistically significant because of the size of sample but they do replicate other findings. The results would seem to indicate that teachers automatically ask more stimulating questions when they are consciously trying to increase student input into discussions.

One of the problems in the research design was that it did not allow for differences in conceptual ability. A teacher automatically adjusts level of questions according

TABLE 2.1

		Think-Time* Seconds	Responses* Words	Level*
Baseline	S1	0.1	2.4	1.2
	S2	1.0	3.5	1.4
Post Test	S1	2.5	4.6	1.5
	S2	3.2	6.3	1.5

* average over ten questions.

to the ability of the group. S2 could not change her level of questions too much because of the conceptual level of the group. S1 had an average group and could, therefore, hope to have higher level responses even though the children were younger.

If I had had more time, I would have analysed far more data for each teacher and increased the number of teachers and done another piece of research to discover if there was any transfer effect using an information-processing model of teaching.

The third example is taken from a paper by Lawrence Stenhouse (1979, 71–77), and reprinted by permission of Universitetsforlaget AS. He describes, in the first person singular, the fictionalised predicament of a teacher who turns to the research literature for advice on which teaching strategy to use.

I teach social studies in the form of human issues programme covering such topics as the family, poverty, people and work, law and order, war and society, relations between the sexes. I wonder whether I should include race relations. A complicating factor is my style of teaching controversial issues to adolescent students. I set up discussions and use evidence such as, newspapers, stories, pamphlets, photographs and films. I act as neutral chairman in those discussions, in order to encourage critical attitudes without taking sides. In short, I have been influenced by and am in the tradition of the English Humanities Curriculum Project (Stenhouse, 1970).

I am very concerned that my teaching should contribute

positively to race relations in my multi-racial society if that is possible. I wonder whether I should teach about race relations at all. If so, I wonder whether it is appropriate in this case to take the role of neutral chairman, even though this is a teaching convention and not a position professing personal neutrality. So I turn to a research report on 'Problems and Effects of Teaching about Race Relations' for enlightenment (*vide,* Stenhouse et al, 1982).

Here I find that the project has monitored on a pre-test, post-test basis two different strategies of teaching about race relations, one in which the teacher is neutral (called Strategy A), the other in which the teacher feels free to express, whenever he feels it appropriate, his committed stance against racism (called Strategy B). Strategy A was conducted in fourteen schools and Stategy B in sixteen schools. The samples are not true random samples because of problems of accessibility of schools and students, but I know something about this from my study of education at college (Campbell and Stanley, 1963). Control groups have been gathered in the same schools as the experimental groups whenever this was possible, though this was not possible in all cases. I came across this table (see Table 2.2) of results on a scale purporting to measure general racism.

This seems to help me a good deal at first sight. My neutral strategy is Strategy A. Attitudes in the Strategy A Group seem to improve and, though the improvement does not quite reach even .05 level of significance, the control groups, left to general influences deteriorate in attitude significantly and the comparison of experimental and control shows at least by one criterion a .01 level discrimination in favour of teaching about race relations by Strategy A. Strategy B does not look markedly superior to Strategy A so I don't seem to need to change my teaching style. So it seems that research has helped me by enabling me to decide the right style in which to teach about race relations.

But, oh dear, here's a problem. On a later page the same data are presented in a different form to show the situation in individual schools and this seems to complicate the issue as shown in Table 2.3.

Now, looking at this table I personally feel that, given

TABLE 2.2 Scores on the general Racism Scale of the Bagley-Verma Test. Decrease in score represents decrease in racism.

Teaching Style	Experimental Sample			Control Sample			Significance of difference ** .01 * .05 and t value for difference of difference Experimental and control
	Pre-test Mean & (S.D.)	Post-test Mean & (S.D.)	Direction of Shift & t value for difference of means	Pre-test Mean & (S.D.)	Post-test Mean & (S.D.)	Direction of shift & t value for difference of means	
Exp. N: 258 Strategy A Control N: 124	17.24 (10.05)	16.51 /10.25)	1.71	16.06 (9.66)	17.61 (10.49)	2.11*	2.83**
Exp. N: 359 Strategy B Control N: 180	17.25 (9.61)	16.17 (9.78)	2.27	17.42 (9.93)	17.87 (10.58)	0.72	1.91

TABLE 2.3 Differences between Pre-test and Post-test School Means for Experimental and Control Groups on the General Racism, Anti-Asian and Anti-Black Scales of the Bagley-Verma Test: Strategy A.

1	2	3	4	5	6	7	8
School Code	Experimental GR	Experimental AA	Experimental AB	Control GR	Control AA	Control AB	Comment Code
03	−1.83	−.35	−1.22	—	—	—	C
07**	1.58	.54	.31	−.86	.21	−.71	G
09	−.22	.55	−.9	2.11	1.45	1.09	A
10*	−.63	−.18	−1.54	—	—	—	C
13	−.85	.37	−1.29	−.89	−.56	−.67	D
17	−2.5	−1.17	−1.78	—	—	—	C
18	1.7	2.4	.9	6.63	4.38	3.75	B
19	.37	−.04	.62	—	—	—	D
29	−3.42	−1.75	−1.67	2.0	.87	−.25	A
31**	−.12	.77	.65	.34	.5	−1.16	D
32**	−1.61	−.7	−.83	−.07	−.77	−.38	A
39*	1.2	−.5	1.05	—	—	—	D
Mean of Strategy A Controls (individuals)				(1.3)	(.83)	(.49)	

** over 25% non-white
* 5–25% non-white

comment codes A, B or C, I certainly ought to proceed, given comment codes D and possibly E I should proceed with great care, and given codes F and G, I might be better to give a lot more thought to the matter. In seven out of twelve schools, the result seems encouraging, in four schools results seem doubtful and in one of the twelve rather alarming. How do I know what category my school will fall into? This is really rather disturbing for my decision. Perhaps I should shift to Strategy B. Let's look at the Strategy B Table – Table 2.4.

Oh dear! This is no better. Here eight out of fifteen schools are reassuring, three are doubtful and three are alarming. Strategy B seems no refuge.

Can it be that statistically significant discriminations between two treatments when presented through means and standard deviations can mask such a range of within sample variance as this? It can indeed. In the psycho-statistical research paradigm, the effects are not 'other things being equal': they are 'by and large' or 'for the most part'. So doing one thing is only sometimes better than doing the other! This apparently depends on your school context or school environment or perhaps yourself or your pupils.

What I have to find out now is whether teaching about race relations by Strategy A is good for my pupils in my school. However, that reminds me that I haven't looked at pupils as individuals, only as means and standard deviations. Suppose I took these data and looked at them in a way that depicted the fate of individuals. How about a histogram of change scores. There are, or course, problems with such scores but, bearing them in mind, I'll give it a go. (See Figure 2.1 and 2.2).

My goodness, it looks as if the same teaching style and the same subject matter make some people worse as they make other people better. One man's meat is another man's poison. If I teach about race relations, some people get worse. But if I refuse to teach about race relations even more people get worse. I suppose I should have thought of that anyway. I know that when I teach literature some people come not to like it, but I believe that even fewer would enjoy literature if I didn't introduce them to it all.

TABLE 2.4 Differences between Pre-test and Post-test School Means for Experimental and Control Groups on the General Racism, Anti-Asian and Anti-Black Scales of the Bagley-Verma Test: Strategy B.

1 School Code	2 Experimental GR	3 Experimental AA	4 Experimental AB	5 Control GR	6 Control AA	7 Control AB	8 Comment Code
01	-3.51	-1.6	-2.57	-1.75	1.43	-1.34	A
02	0	-.67	-.10	2.43	1.22	1.43	A
04*	1.04	.10	.24	—	—	—	E
05	-2.27	-.34	-.97	—	—	—	C
06*	-2.00	1.29	-1.30	.55	.34	-.52	D
08	1.09	.30	.07	-5.4	-1.2	-2.33	G
09	-2.89	-.22	-1.97	2.11	1.45	1.09	A
11	-1.58	-.48	-.53	—	—	—	C
14**	-.33	.39	.91	—	—	—	D
15	-2.25	.17	-1.42	—	—	—	C
20	-.39	.05	-.22	-1.15	.86	-1.43	F
21	-1.77	-1.32	-1.19	1.59	1.04	.59	A
24*	.19	.37	.60	4.93	1.07	1.65	B
30*	3.79	1.27	2.16	—	—	—	E
33	1.00	.43	.38	-.83	.83	-.08	G
Mean of Strategy B Controls (individuals)				.90	.71	.30	

** over 25% non-white
* 5–25% non-white

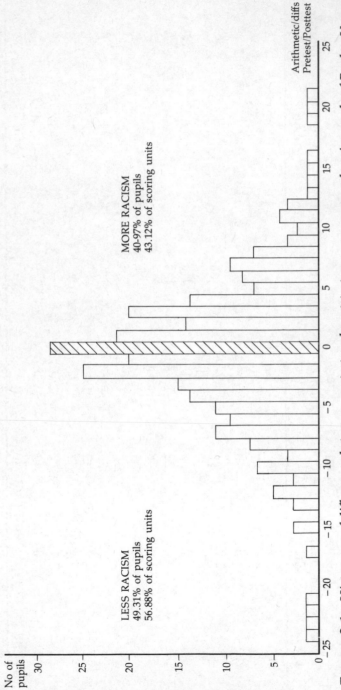

FIGURE 2.1 *Histogram of differences between pre-test and post-test scores on general racism scale of Bagley-Verma test: strategy A experimental (N = 288)*

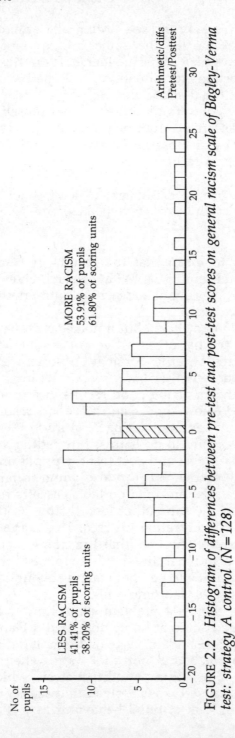

FIGURE 2.2 *Histogram of differences between pre-test and post-test scores on general racism scale of Bagley-Verma test: strategy A control (N=128)*

I need to steady myself. After all, engineers don't always build exactly the same bridge. Nor do chess players always play the same game. There must be ways of fitting action to situation and perhaps even to individuals in that situation.

I've clearly got to think things out for myself. Does this mean that research cannot help me? What was that piece in the paper by Cronbach they gave us in Ed. Psych? Here are my notes. And here it is:

> When we give proper weight to local conditions, any generalization is a working hypothesis, not a conclusion. (Cronbach, 1975: 125).

That seems to mean that the results of research need testing in local conditions. What research gives me is most often not findings about all teaching but hypotheses about my teaching.

This is a bit of a shock, but it makes reasonable enough sense. And the hypotheses I've got are already of some use. I must test whether Strategy A works well for me in my classroom, whether I can sustain its logic in practice and whether it is giving good results in attitudes. At the same time, I know that even in a good result some individuals may be deteriorating in attitude.

What I am going to do is this. I'm getting a student to come in and pre-test and post-test my pupils and a control group in my school. But I'm also going to tape our sessions on race relations on a portable cassette recorder. To do this, I have to tape other lessons too, so that I don't seem to be concentrating on race. I've started this. I'm explaining to the students that I'm doing a study of my own teaching and that this should help me to teach better. And I'm beginning to get them talking about how well my teaching and their learning goes.

Of course, there's a problem about how to handle the tapes. I played some at home and tried a Flanders Interaction Analysis (Flanders, 1970) on them. It did tell me that I talked too much, but not a lot more. Then I tried the Humanities Curriculum Project analysis which worked quite well because I was involved in discussion teaching. But I want to look at pupil behaviour as well as teacher behaviour. I'm beginning to ask myself whether I can develop a theory of individuals who cause me concern in class. I don't even need paper to do that. I can play cassettes in my car as I drive to and from work.

The more I come to study my own classroom, and my own school as well, the more I come to understand why the research provides case studies of classrooms. Comparing other people's experiences with my own throws up all sorts of illuminating possibilities – hypotheses, I mean.

At the end of this session, I'm going to try to set up a club in the district for teacher–researchers. They have clubs for people who tinker with motor cycles to get more performance from them: why not the same for teachers who are tinkering with their teaching?

I'd like to set about testing Piaget. Most of his experiments are a kind of teaching. And I have a feeling that if I work with a small sample, like he did, I'll find out quite a lot for myself. I've got a better laboratory than he had: it's a real classroom!

I'm not sure if I'm doing research. I am testing hypothesis by experiment as systematically as a busy job allows.

The Shorter Oxford English Dictionary says that research is: 'Investigation, inquiry into things. Also, habitude of carrying out such investigation.' Well, it is beginning to become a habit.

Commentary

These examples give a flavour of teachers doing research in their classrooms, and they will be referred to as illustrative cases later. Although the substance of the research undertaken in the examples differs, each of them shows teachers engaging in systematic self-conscious enquiry in order to understand and improve practice. In reflecting on the examples, it may be useful to consider how far they reflect your own experience or that of your colleagues. Although each of the examples is an instance of classroom research by teachers, there are significant differences (aside from the focus of their enquiries) in the style of the individual research efforts. Can you identify ways in which the approaches to classroom research by teachers in the examples differ?

Further Reading

There are a number of sources for further examples of classroom research by teachers. In *A Teacher's Guide to Action Research*, Jon Nixon (1981), presents a series of descriptive accounts by teachers of a variety of classroom research projects. Extended illustrations of teacher research are given by Michael Armstrong (1980) in *Closely Observed Children* and Stephen Rowland (1984) in *The Enquiring Classroom*. A classic example of classroom research in this tradition, although it also involved the participation of an external researcher, is found in Smith and Geoffrey's (1986) *The Complexities of an Urban Classroom*. Jean Rudduck and her colleagues (*vide*, Rudduck, 1981, May and Rudduck, 1983, Hull *et al*. 1985) have produced collections of teacher research accounts as a result of their funded research projects. The Classroom Action Research Network (CARN) publish an annual bulletin that serves as a forum for teachers to publish accounts of their classroom research activities. The Ford Teaching Project materials also contain a series of case studies of teacher research, as do the recent books on the Teacher–Pupil Interaction and the Quality Of Learning (TIQL) project by Elliott and Ebbutt (1985a, b) and Ebbutt and Elliott (1985) (The CARN Ford Teaching Project, and TIQL Project material can be obtained from the Cambridge Institute of Education, address in Appendix A).

3

Why Classroom Research by Teachers?

In asking the question, 'Why classroom research by teachers?', one is raising a whole series of issues around the topics of professionalism, teacher behaviour, the social control of teachers and the utility of educational research. Each of these issues provides a rationale for teacher research. For example, classroom research by teachers can be justified by reference to professionalism because systematic self study is a hallmark of those occupations that enjoy the label 'professional'. Unfortunately the teachers' claim to professionalism falters at this definition. In this chapter however, I want to focus on two other issues. First is the link between classroom research by teachers and the establishing and refining of professional judgement. Second, I will explore some of the impediments in the traditional approach to educational research.

'Autonomous in Professional Judgement'

Lawrence Stenhouse (1984, 69) described the ideal role of the teacher like this:

> Good teachers are necessarily autonomous in professional judgement. They do not need to be told what to do. They

are not professionally the dependents of researchers or superintendents, of innovators or supervisors. This does not mean that they do not welcome access to ideas created by other people at other places or in other times. Nor do they reject advice, consultancy or support. But they do know that ideas and people are not of much real use until they are digested to the point where they are subject to the teacher's own judgement. In short, it is the task of all educationalists outside the classroom to serve the teachers; for only teachers are in the position to create good teaching.

This is a very different image from the contemporary linear approach to schooling that is based on the assumption that instructions issued from the top, from the minister, the director or principal, are put into practice at the appropriate level lower down the organizational structure. Consequently, our systems of schooling are much like factories which operate on a rational input–output basis, with pupils as raw material, teachers as mechanics, the curriculum as the productive process, and the school administrators as factory managers.

The reaction to this popular and tacit concept of schooling encouraged the development of the teacher research movement. John Elliott (in Nixon 1981, 1) has observed that 'the teacher as researcher movement emanated from the work and ideas of Lawrence Stenhouse'. Crucial to an understanding of Stenhouse's intellectual position is, as we saw in chapter one, the notion of emancipation (*vide*, Stenhouse, 1983). In this context, emancipation refers to the process involved in liberating teachers from a system of education that denies individual dignity by returning to them some degree of self worth through the exercise of professional judgement. In terms of curriculum and teaching, the path to emancipation involves reconceptualizing curriculum development as curriculum research, and the linking of research to the art of teaching (Rudduck and Hopkins, 1985). When viewed through this particular lens, approaches such as the use of behavioural objectives for curriculum planning become prescriptive blue prints that tend to inhibit autonomy in teaching and learning.

The experimental or process model of curriculum, such as used in HCP, is liberating or emancipatory because it encourages independence of thought and argument on the part of the pupil, and experimentation and the use of judgement on the part of the teacher. This attitude encourages not only new pedagogic roles for the teacher, but implies a different way of viewing knowledge. In this situation, no longer is knowledge given or absolute, the teacher treats it hypothetically and the pupils enhance their own authority through its use.

When teachers adopt this experimental approach to their teaching they are taking on an educational idea, cast in the form of a curriculum proposal, and testing it within their classrooms. As Stenhouse (1975, 142) said:

> The crucial point is that the proposal is not to be regarded as an unqualified recommendation but rather as a provisional specification claiming no more than to be worth putting to the test of practice. Such proposals claim to be intelligent rather than correct.

Alternatively, the teacher may be genuinely interested in disclosing to him or herself some of the dynamics of their classroom or to evaluate certain aspects of their own teaching style. In each of these situations, the teacher is engaging in classroom research for the express purpose of improving the quality of educational life in that classroom.

The motivation for doing so may be varied – a research degree, natural curiosity, a stimulating article or talk – but the process and its implications are essentially the same. The major consequence being that teachers take more control of their professional lives. Not content to be told what to do or being uncertain about what it is one is doing, teachers who engage in their own research are developing their professional judgement and are moving towards emancipation and autonomy.

I am calling this form of research in which teachers do research in their own classrooms for the purpose of improving practice, teacher research. The phrase, teacher research, has the advantage of being simple and identifies the major actor and the process involved. It is in this sense and with this aspiration that the terms 'classroom research by teachers', 'teacher-based research' and the 'teacher–researcher' are used in this book.

Problems in Traditional Approaches

The most unfortunate aspect of traditional educational research is that it is extremely difficult to apply its findings to classroom practice. The third case study in chapter two is a good illustration of this. In a quandary about which teaching strategy to use the fictionalised teacher went to the research literature for guidance. His subsequent experience was as frustrating as it was predictable, because the literature contains few unequivocal signposts for action. This dilemma is widespread: teachers quite rightly (in most cases) regard educational research as something irrelevant to their lives and see little interaction between the world of the educational researcher and the world of the teacher.

Arthur Bolster (1983, 295) asks the question 'Why has research on teaching had so little influence on practice?', and his response to the question is worth quoting:

> The major reason, in my opinion, is that most such research, especially that emanating from top-ranked schools of education, construes teaching from a theoretical perspective that is incompatible with the perspective teachers must employ in thinking about their work. In other words, researchers and school teachers adopt radically different sets of assumptions about how to conceptualize the teaching process. As a result, the conclusions of much formal research on teaching appear irrelevant to classroom teachers – not necessarily wrong, just not very sensible or useful. If researchers are to generate knowledge that is likely to affect classroom practice, they must construe their inquiries in ways that are much more compatible with teachers' perspectives.

Most researchers when they enter classrooms bring with them perspectives derived from academic disciplines. Their view of how knowledge evolves and how it is determined are firmly established by their formal training. The world view that guides researchers' actions is consequently at odds with that of teachers. The teacher derives his or her knowledge of teaching from continual participation in situational decision making and the classroom culture in which they and their pupils live out their daily lives. So one reason why traditional educational research is of little use to the teachers is because of the differing conceptions of teaching held by teachers and researchers. But there are other problems. Research in education is usually carried out within the psycho-statistical research paradigm. This implies tightly controlled experimentation and the testing of hypotheses by assessing the effectiveness of a treatment across randomly selected groups through the use of statistical analysis. This approach is based on the agricultural research designs of R. A. Fisher (1935) in the 1930s. At that time, educationalists, desiring to link research to action, began to utilize the very successful 'agricultural–botany' designs of Fisher in educational settings. This has continued (and increased) down to the present day as can be seen by the myriad of postgraduate theses that use this research design. The basic idea underlying Fisher's designs is that experiments are conducted on samples, usually divided into a control and an experimental group, with the results generalized to the target population. The point is that samples are randomly drawn and are consequently representative of that target population.

Stenhouse (1979) describes Fisher's approach like this:

> The strength of Fisher's paradigm is the recognition of random sampling, in which a sample is drawn such that each member of the target population has an equal chance of being included in the sample because it is a device of chance....
>
> In Fisher's agricultural setting, the hypotheses were not derived from scientific theory.... They were hypotheses regarding the relative effectiveness of alternative procedures, and the criteria of effectiveness was gross crop yield.
>
> The result of an experiment of this kind is an estimate of the probability that – other things being equal – a particular seed strain or fertilizer or amount of watering will result in a higher gross yield than an alternative against which it has been tested... It is in applying experimental methods to teaching and curriculum evaluation in the schools that researchers have used the Fisherian model. The assumption is that one teaching procedure or curriculum can be tested against alternatives as a seed strain or fertilizer can in agriculture, i.e. procedures can be tested against yield without a real theoretical framework.

This approach to educational research is problematic, particulary if its results are to be applied to classrooms. First of all, it is extraordinarily difficult to draw random samples in educational settings (e.g. a random sample of schools, pupils and teachers would have to be drawn separately). Second, there are a myriad of contextual variables operating on schools and classrooms (e.g. community culture, teacher personality, school ethos, socioeconomic background, etc.) that would affect the results. Third, it is difficult to establish criteria for effective classroom or school performance. Even if one could resolve these difficulties there are, as Stenhouse (1979) points out, two deeper problems that relate to the nature of educational activity.

First, the 'agricultural – botany' paradigm is based on measures of gross yield (i.e. how much produce can be gathered in total from a section of land). That is an inappropriate measure for education. As teachers, we are concerned with the individual progress of students rather than with aggregated scores from the class or the school. Our emphasis is on varying teaching methods to suit individual pupils in order to help them achieve to the limit of their potential. Stenhouse (1979, 79) puts the paradox like this:

> The teacher is like a gardener who treats different plants differently, and not like a large scale farmer who administers standardised treatments to as near as possible standardised plants.

The second deeper problem relates to meaningful action. The teacher–pupil or pupil–pupil interactions that result in effective learning are not so much the consequence of a standardized teaching method but the result of both teachers and pupils engaging in meaningful action. And meaningful action cannot be standardized by control or sample. This is a similar argument to the one commonly used against those who overrate the utility of behavioural objectives. Behavioural objectives provide an excellent means for the teaching of skills or evaluating rote learning, but they tend to be counter-productive with more complex and sophisticated content areas. In the instance of rote learning, one can accept the parallel with standardized treatments, but not so easily with poetry appreciation. Here pupil response is the result of individual negotiation with the subject, mediated through and by the teacher – namely a form of meaningful action. In this case, education as induction into knowledge is successful to the extent that it makes the behavioural outcomes of pupils unpredictable and therefore, not generalizable. The implications of this line of thinking for teacher-researchers is to encourage them to look outside the psycho-statistical paradigm for their research procedures.

To summarize, I have made two points in arguing that the traditional approach to educational research is not of much use to teachers. The first point is that teachers and researchers do not conceptualize teaching in the same way. They live in different intellectual worlds and so their meanings rarely connect. Second, the usual form of educational research, the psysco-statistical or agricultural–botany paradigm, has severe limitations as a method of construing and making sense of classroom reality. For these two reasons, teachers and those concerned with understanding classroom life have increasingly adopted different approaches to classroom research.

Arthur Bolster (1983) advocates an ethnographic approach as the research methodology most likely to generate knowledge that is intellectually rigorous and helpful for teacher development. Stenhouse goes further than this and suggests not only a research approach that is grounded in the reality of classroom culture but one that is under the control of teachers. It is the description of such an approach to classroom research that provides the substance of the following chapter.

Commentary

In this chapter , I have discussed two themes that justify and, indeed, make imperative a concept of classroom research by teachers. The first argument has to do with the nature of professionalism in teaching, and the second, with the inappropriateness of the traditional research paradigm for helping teachers improve their teaching. As you reflect on these arguments and test their authenticity against your experience, it may be useful to ask yourself questions such as 'How "emancipated" am I as a teacher?', How far am I encouraged by my Head/Principal or my Local Education Authority to become "autonomous in professional judgement?"' 'How often do I talk about my teaching to colleagues on staff?' And in connection with research, 'How useful have I found educational research in helping me to improve my teaching?' 'How appropriate are experimental or quasi-experimental research designs to my teaching situation?'

Further Reading

The notion of professionalism used in this chapter comprises a major theme in two of Lawrence Stenhouse's books: *An Introduction to Curriculum Research and Development* (1975) and *Authority, Education and Emancipation* (1983). An important discussion of the nature of teacher professionalism is included in Dan Lortie's (1975) *School Teacher*. An excellent wide ranging discussion of the practical implications of professionalism is found in Donald Schon's (1983)*The Reflective Practitioner*. For a more detailed exposition of Stenhouse's critique of the traditional approach to educational research see *Research as a Basis for Teaching* (Rudduck and Hopkins 1985). An entertaining and comprehensive review of the arguments against traditional educational research as well as an alternative approach is found in *Beyond the Numbers Game* (Hamilton *et al.* 1977).

4

Action Research and Classroom Research by Teachers

In the previous chapter, I outlined a series of problems associated with the traditional approach to educational research that limits its usefulness for teachers who wish to improve their practice. There are, however, at least two other research traditions to which teachers can turn. One tradition is associated with the work of sociologists and anthropoligists. Social-anthropological, ethnographic, phenomenological, naturalistic and illuminative research are examples of these research approaches. These are long words that describe essentially the same approach; one that attempts to understand a social situation and to derive hypotheses from that effort of appreciation. The procedures that such social scientists have developed for analysing fieldwork data are used in this book as a guide for making sense of classroom data. These are described in some detail in chapter eight.

The other research tradition that stands in contrast to the psycho-statistical paradigm and has a strong link with contemporary social science research is a method known as action research. In recent years, teacher–researchers have adopted the label action research to describe their particular approach to classroom research. In this chapter I describe and critique this application of action research, and from the discussion propose five criteria for classroom research by teachers.

Action Research

Action research combines a substantive act with a research procedure; it is action disciplined by enquiry, a personal attempt at understanding whilst engaged in a process of improvement and reform.

Here are three definitions of action research. The first is by Rapoport (1970) who says that action research:

> ... aims to contribute both to the practical concerns of people in an immediate problematic situation and to the goals of social science by joint collaboration within a mutually acceptable ethical framework.

The second is by Stephen Kemmis (1983) who writes:

> Action research is a form of self-reflective enquiry under-taken by participants in social (including educational) situations in order to improve the rationality and justice of (a) their own social or educational practices, (b) their understanding of these practices, and (c) the situations in which the practices are carried out. It is most rationally empowering when undertaken by participants collabor-atively, though it is often undertaken by individuals, and sometimes in cooperation with 'outsiders'. In education, action research has been employed in school-based cur-riculum development, professional development, school improvement programs, and systems planning and policy development.

The third is taken from a paper by Dave Ebbutt (1983) who not only gives a definition of his own, but also quotes from Elliott and Kemmis. He writes that action research:

> ... is about the systematic study of attempts to improve educational practice by groups of participants by means of their own practical actions and by means of their own reflection upon the effects of those actions.

... is the study of a social situation with a view to improving quality of action within it. (Elliott).

Put simply action research is the way groups of people can organise the conditions under which they can learn from their own experience. (Kemmis)

Action research is trying out an idea in practice with a view to improving or changing something, trying to have a real effect on the situation. (Kemmis)

The idea of action research was developed by Kurt Lewin in the immediate post-war period as a method of intervening into social problems. Lewin identified four phrases to action research – planning, acting, observing, and reflecting; and envisaged it being based on principles that could lead 'gradually to independence, equality and cooperation' (Lewin, 1946).

The combination of the action and the research components has a powerful appeal for teachers; Lawrence Stenhouse was quick to point to the connection between action research and his concept of the teacher as researcher. Later, John Elliott popularized action research as a method for teachers doing research in their own classrooms through the Ford Teaching Project, and established the Classroom Action Research Network.

Models of Action Research

Recently Stephen Kemmis has considerably refined and formalized the concept of action research and how it applies to education. Based at Deakin University in Australia, Kemmis has produced a series of publications and courses and materials on action research, curriculum development and evaluation based on the Open University model. His article on action research (Kemmis, 1983) is a useful review of how educational action research has developed from the work of Lewin and established its own character. Of more interest to us is his *Action Research Planner* (Kemmis and McTaggart, 1981) where a sequential programme for teachers intending to engage in action research is outlined in some detail. He summarizes his approach to action research in the model shown in Figure 4.1.

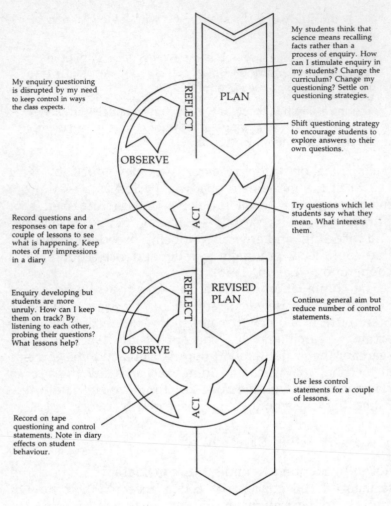

My students think that science means recalling facts rather than a process of enquiry. How can I stimulate enquiry in my students? Change the curriculum? Change my questioning? Settle on questioning strategies.

My enquiry questioning is disrupted by my need to keep control in ways the class expects.

Shift questioning strategy to encourage students to explore answers to their own questions.

REFLECT

PLAN

OBSERVE

ACT

Try questions which let students say what they mean. What interests them.

Record questions and responses on tape for a couple of lessons to see what is happening. Keep notes of my impressions in a diary

Enquiry developing but students are more unruly. How can I keep them on track? By listening to each other, probing their questions? What lessons help?

REFLECT

REVISED PLAN

Continue general aim but reduce number of control statements.

OBSERVE

ACT

Use less control statements for a couple of lessons.

Record on tape questioning and control statements. Note in diary effects on student behaviour.

FIGURE 4.1 *Action research in action*

John Elliott was quick to take up Kemmis' schema of the action research spiral and he, too, produced a similar but more elaborate model as seen in Figure 4.2. Elliott (1981) summarizes Kemmis' approach and then outlines his elaborations like this:

> Although I think Kemmis' model is an excellent basis for starting to think about what action research involves, it can allow those who use it to assume that 'The General Idea' can be fixed in advance, that 'Reconnaissance' is merely

fact-finding, and that 'Implementation' is a fairly straight forward process. But I would argue that:

'The General Idea' should be allowed to shift.

'Reconnaissance' should involve analysis as well as fact finding, and should constantly recur in the spiral of activities, rather than occur only at the beginning.

'Implementation' of an action-step is not always easy, and one should not proceed to evaluate the effects of an action until one has monitored the extent to which it has been implemented.

Dave Ebbutt (1983), a colleague of Elliott provides us with another variation on Kemmis' model and makes these comments about it:

It seems clear to me that Elliott is wrong in one respect, in suggesting that Kemmis equates reconnaissance with fact finding only. The Kemmis diagram clearly shows reconnaissance to comprise discussing, negotiating, exploring opportunities, assessing possibilities and examining constraints – in short there are elements of analysis in the Kemmis notion of reconnaissance. Nevertheless I suggest that the thrust of Elliott's three statements is an attempt on the part of a person experienced in directing action research projects to recapture some of the 'messiness' of the action-research cycle which the Kemmis version tends to gloss.

But Ebbutt (1983) claims that the spiral is not the most useful metaphor; instead the most

... appropriate way to conceive of the process of action research is to think of it as comprising of a series of successive cycles, each incorporating the possibility for the feedback of information within and between cycles. Such a description is not nearly so neat as conceiving of the process as a spiral, neither does it lend itself quite so tidily to a diagrammatic representation. In my view the idealized process of educational action research can be more appropriately represented like this: [as shown in Figure 4.3]

My purpose in presenting these three models of action research is to provide an overview of action research to

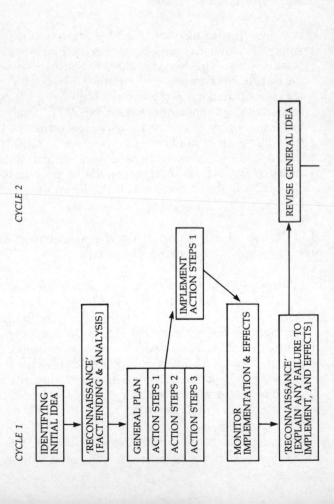

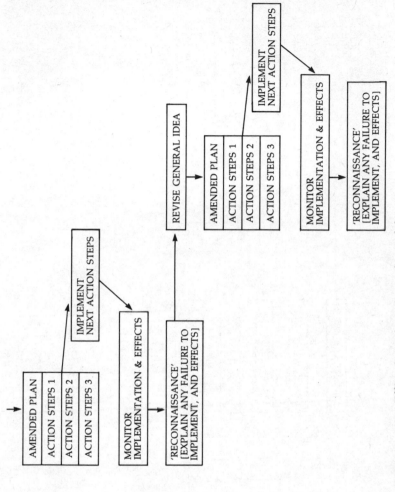

FIGURE 4.2 *Elliott's action research model*

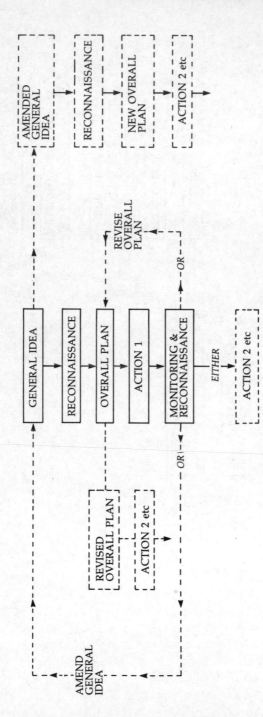

Idealized Representation of the Process of Action Research

FIGURE 4.3   *Ebbutt's model*

help the reader gain an understanding of the whole process. There are, however, some problems inherent in these models and to these I now turn.

Critique of Educational Action Research

There are two main areas of concern that I have with the action research models developed by Kemmis, Elliott and Ebbutt. Although this is not the place for a thoroughgoing critique, a brief discussion of these concerns is necessary because the problems may lead teacher–researchers into possible confusion. Also, the critique will help explain the form and structure of the rest of the book.

My first concern is that there may be a misunderstanding of the nature of Lewinian action research. As I mentioned earlier, the term action research was coined as a useful label to describe what teacher–researchers were doing. Recently, much energy has been devoted to setting out the intellectual basis for action research as it derived from Lewin. This energy has been misplaced because Lewin's conception of action research is very different from what goes on in the name of teacher research. Lewin's concept of action research was (i) as an externally initiated intervention designed to assist a client system, (ii) functionalist in orientation, and (iii) prescriptive in practice. None of these features apply to what I assume to be the nature of classroom research by teachers which is characterized by its practitioner, problem solving, and eclectic orientation.

I am also concerned about the values implicit in the Lewinian approach. The functionalist values that appear in his writing tend to offset his commitment to democratic and communitarian values. It is doubly ironic that Kemmis illustrates the process of action research by citing Lewin's example of the bombing of German factories! Although Kemmis says that educational action research has moved away from Lewin's original ideas, I am still concerned that this emphasis will associate teacher research with a set of values that are at odds with its central emphasis on individual autonomy, action and 'emancipation'. What began as a useful label to describe a loose set of activities undertaken for professional development purposes is in danger of assuming a rather different character as a result of a quest for intellectual credibility.

My other concern relates to the specification of process in the action research models. There are three interelated points. The first is that the tight specification of process steps and cycles may trap teachers within a framework which they may come to depend on and which will consequently inhibit independent action. The original purpose of teacher research was to free teachers from the constraints of prespecified research designs. It is useful to have a guide for action, my concern is when it becomes, or appears to become, prescriptive. Second, the models outline a process rather than a technology. They delineate a sequence of stages, but say little about the 'what' and the 'how' within these stages. Third, the models may appear daunting and confusing to practitioners. Ebbutt himself admits that the Elliott framework tends to mystification.

Unfortunately models and frameworks cannot mirror reality: they are one individual's interpretation of reality. Consequently, they impose upon the user a prespecified analysis of a process that the user may quite rightly interpret differently. At best, they provide a starting point, an initial guide to action. At worst, they trap the practitioners within a set of assumptions that bear little relationship to their reality and, consequently, constrain their freedom of action.

Classroom Research by Teachers

I prefer to talk about 'classroom research by teachers' rather than 'action research'. Instead of producing an elaborate step by step model, I will present a series of methods and techniques that teachers can use in their classroom research efforts. In particular, I will discuss:

1. ways in which classroom research projects can be identified and initiated (chapter five)

2. methods of gathering data on classroom behaviours (chapters six and seven)

3. ways of interpreting and analysing the data gathered from classroom research (chapter eight)

4. ways in which the research process can be sustained (chapter nine).

My purpose in tackling classroom research in this way is to give teachers an introduction to the variety of methods available to them as a means of extending their repertoire of professional behaviours and of encouraging flexibility in professional development. These are methods and approaches that teachers can put into use, that will empower them, and make them increasingly competent and 'autonomous in professional judgement'.

Criteria for Classroom Research by Teachers

The essence of what I am advocating is the development of a teacher's professional expertise and judgement. Although many teachers are in broad agreement with this general aim, some are quite rightly concerned about how far involvement in classroom research activity will impinge upon their teaching and on their personal time. Concerns are also raised as to the utilitarian or practical value of classroom research. With these concerns in mind, let me suggest the following five principles for classroom research by teachers.

The first is that the teacher's primary job is to teach, and any research method should not interfere with or disrupt the teaching commitment. This rule of thumb should serve to quell immediate concerns, but it also points to certain ethical considerations. In some instances, it may be inevitable that the adoption of a new and barely internalized teaching strategy is initially less effective than the way one previously taught. Is it ethical, therefore, some may ask, for a teacher to subject students to an inferior performance when the original behaviour was perfectly adequate? These are questions which ultimately can only be answered by the individuals involved. For my part, I am prepared to stand behind the teacher's judgement, particularly if the teachers involved are so concerned about improving the teaching and the learning experience of their students that they have broken the mould and are experimenting with new models. In becoming a teacher–researcher, the individual teacher is deliberately and consciously expanding his or her role to include a professional element. It is almost inconceivable then that he or she would do this and at the same time ignore the primacy of the teaching/learning act.

The second criterion is that the method of data collection must not be too demanding on the teacher's time. As a corollary, the teacher needs to be certain about the data collection technique before using it. The reasons for this are obvious. Teachers already consider themselves over-worked and there are continuing demands for increased preparation and professional development time. It is naive to assume that the adoption of a research role will make no inroads on a teacher's private time. This can be re-duced, however, by judicious use of specific data collec-tion techniques, and the utilization of easily analysed diagnostic methods. For example, the tape recorder is widely regarded as a very useful tool for the classroom researcher. It is, however, extremely expensive to use both in terms of time and money. It takes approximately 50% longer to listen to a tape than to make it, and on top of that transcription (which is necessary if full use is to be made of the method) is both time consuming or expen-sive. Given this, it is advisable to use another method for broad spectrum diagnosis and reserve such intensive techniques for specific and finely focused enquiries. A taxonomy of data collection techniques is presented in chapter six, and in chapter seven a number of techniques for classroom observation are discussed.

The third criterion is perhaps the most contentious. The methodology employed must be reliable enough to allow teachers to formulate hypotheses confidently and develop strategies applicable to their classroom situation. Tradi-tional researchers hold a poor opinion of action research. In many cases, that opinion is well founded particularly if it is based on individual pieces of research. It behoves all researchers, be they psycho-statisticians engaged in large scale research or a primary teacher testing Piaget's theoretical hypotheses, to be rigorous about their methodology. It is no excuse at all to claim that rigour is unnecessary because the research is practitioner oriented, small scale, or used solely to improve individual practice. If a change in teaching strategy is to be made, then that decision needs to be based on reliable data. These issues form the substance of chapter eight.

The fourth criterion is that the research problem undertaken by the teacher should be one to which he or she is committed. Although this sounds self-evident, it is difficult enough, given all the pressures on a teacher's time, to sustain energy in a project even if it is intrinsically interesting and important to the teachers' professional activities. As a corollary, the problem must in fact be a problem; that is, the problem must be capable of solution, else by definition it is not a problem. If a teacher chooses a topic that is too complex or amorphous then frustration and disillusionment will soon set in.

The fifth criterion refers to the need for teacher–researchers to pay close attention to the ethical procedures surrounding their work. Ethical standards for classroom researchers have been worked out over the past decade by researchers associated with the Centre for Applied Research in Education (e.g. Macdonald and Walker, 1974 Simons 1982). A summary of ethical procedures for teacher–researchers is found in Appendix B.

In the chapters that follow, these criteria will be dealt with in more detail. In the next chapter, problem formation and the ways to initiate classroom research projects are discussed.

Commentary

In this chapter, I have discussed and critiqued the concept of educational action research. The importance of action research is not to be underestimated, because it provides teachers with a legitimate and more appropriate alternative to traditional research designs. And in its present form, it also provides a guide to action. We must, however, be aware of the problems associated with too prescriptive a framework for action, and the values that are embedded within it.

The line between specifying principles of procedure that encourage informed action, and prescribing activities that determine behaviour and limit outcomes, is a very fine one indeed. There is a real danger that teacher research will assume the character of the objectives model which:

> ... is like a site-plan simplified so that people know exactly where to dig their trenches without having to know why (Stenhouse 1980).

To use Jean Rudduck's felicitous phrase, it seems that already 'the elusive butterfly of teacher research has been caught and pinned'. Consequently I propose using terms like 'classroom research by teachers'. This implies the acquisition of skills and techniques that become part of a teachers' repertoire and are subject to the exercise of their professional judgement.

In reflecting on this chapter, it may be useful to consider the differences between the psycho-statistical paradigm and teacher based research approaches; and to evaluate in terms of your own experience the usefulness of the action research frameworks and my critique of them.

Further Reading

One of the early examples of teacher based research was the Humanities Curriculum Project and the approach is worth considering (e.g. Stenhouse, 1970). Of similar interest are the early accounts of the Ford Teaching Project (Elliott and Adelman, 1976). There are a number of well known articles on Lewinian action research which, although rather technical and specialized, may be of interest (vide, Lewin, 1946, Rapoport, 1970, Sandford, 1970). Of more immediate concern is the work of Kemmis. His article on action research (Kemmis, 1983) provides an excellent overview of the topic, and the Action Research Planner (Kemmis and McTaggart, 1981) not only contains a step-by-step guide, but also a useful introductory essay on action research. The papers by Elliott (1981) and Ebbutt

(1983) extend Kemmis' work, all of which are critiqued in a rather polemical article by Hopkins (1984a). Background reading on the teacher–researcher movement and its educational context is found in Stenhouse (1975) *An Introduction to Curriculum Research and Development*, and in Carr and Kemmis (1983) *Becoming Critical*.

5

Problem Formation

Engaging in classroom research is initially often an unnerving and occasionally threatening experience. Trying anything new involves uncertainty and this is particularly true of teacher research, especially when the school environment is not supportive of professional development. It is important that the fourth criterion mentioned in the previous chapter – that of identifying and being committed to a topic for classroom research which is stated in workable terms – is adhered to. In this chapter, I will review some ways in which teachers can formulate problems for classroom research, establish hypotheses and engage in theorizing. In short, this chapter deals with how to get started on classroom research.

Problem Identification

This subheading is somewhat misleading for, as Kemmis and McTaggart (1981, 18) point out in *The Action Research Planner*:

> You do not have to begin with a 'problem'. All you need is a general idea that something might be improved. Your general idea may stem from a promising new idea or the recognition that existing practice falls short of aspiration. In either case you must centre attention on:

- What is happening now?
- In what sense is this problematic?
- What can I do about it?

     General starting points will look like –

- I would like to improve the...
- Some people are unhappy about...
- What can I do to change the situation?
- I am perplexed by...
- ...is a source of irritation. What can I do about it?
- I have an idea I would like to try out in my class.
- How can the experience of ... be applied to...?
- Just what do I do with respect to...?

As you read the extract, no doubt certain ideas or topics for classroom research come to mind. It is worth taking a few minutes to jot down these ideas; don't worry about how well they are formed, at this stage it is more important to generate a list of topics from which one can work. Having produced a list, the next step is to evaluate the usefulness, viability and/or importance of the individual topic. There are a number of guidelines that you can use here.

First, do not tackle issues that you cannot do anything about. For example, it may be impossible in the short or medium term, to alter the banding or streaming system in your school or to change the textbook that you are using. Because you cannot do anything about it, either avoid the issue or rephrase it in a more solvable form. So, although you cannot change the textbook, it may be possible to experiment with different ways the text could be used as evidence in your classes.

Second, only take on, at least initially, small scale and relatively limited topics. There are several reasons for this. It is important to build on success, and a small scale project satisfactorily completed in a short space of time is reinforcing and encouraging. It is also very easy to underestimate the scale and amount of time a project will take. It is very discouraging to have found after the initial flush of enthusiasm that you have bitten off more than you can chew.

Third, choose a topic that is important to you or to your students, or one that you have to be involved with anyway in the course of your normal school activities. The topic that you focus on needs to be intrinsically motivating. If not, then again after the initial flush of enthusiasm and when the difficulties begin to build up, you will find that motivation will begin to evaporate.

In summary, then, when choosing a topic for classroom research make certain, at least initially, that it is viable, discrete and intrinsically interesting.

Performance Gap

A growing body of research suggests, 1. there is often incongruence between a teacher's publicly declared philosophy or beliefs about education and how he or she behaves in the classroom, 2. there is often incongruence between the teacher's declared goals and objectives and the way in which the lesson is actually taught, and 3. there is often a discrepancy between a teacher's perceptions or account of a lesson, and the perceptions or account of other participants (e.g. pupils or observers) in the classroom (*vide*, Elbaz, 1983). All of these discrepancies reflect a gap between behaviour and intention and are a source for classroom research problems. The Ford Teaching Project, for example, monitored the performance gap between teacher's aspirations and their practice.

Dave Ebbutt (1983) writes about 'the performance gap' as follows:

> It is via the notion of a performance gap – a gap between espoused theory and theory in action – by which advocates of action research locate its niche as an appropriate mode of research in schools and classrooms. For instance Kemmis in his *Planner* uses this illustrative example:
>
>> There is a gap between the idea and the reality of inquiry teaching in my own classroom. Recognising this gap, I must develop a strategy of action if improvements in this kind of questioning are to be achieved...

If you now return to the list of possible classroom research topics that you have just generated, there is probably implicit in each of the topics a description of what is currently happening (that provides a basis for reflection) and an indication of some new action connected to the existing behaviour that will lead to improvement. So, for example, in the case studies in chapter two, the teachers identified an existing teaching behaviour and at the same time thought of ways in which this aspect of their teaching could be improved. It is this gap between what is and what could be that is an important source of motivation in classroom research by teachers.

Ebbutt (1983) also illustrates the notion of the performance gap by reference to the Open University course *Curriculum in Action*. Here the course team are concerned with demonstrating the gap between the curriculum in action and the curriculum as intention. They do this by posing six simple questions:

1. What did the pupils actually do?
2. What were they learning?
3. How worthwhile was it?
4. What did I do?
5. What did I learn?
6. What do I intend to do now?

The concept of the performance gap is useful in refining your list of topics for classroom research. The identification of a gap between what is and what could be provides motivation for change and indicates a direction for improvement. Action leads out of existing behaviours towards a new articulated goal.

Open and Closed Problems

Implicit in much of what I have written so far is the idea that problems emerge out of a teacher's critical reflection on classroom experience, and then are explored through the use of the classroom research procedures. In other words, both problem formation and problem resolution are grounded in teacher experience.

Problem formation occurs within an open or closed context. Open problems take as their starting point a teacher's critical reflection on his or her teaching: this reflection culminates in a decision to utilize classroom research techniques to understand more fully and then improve his or her teaching (using the techniques discussed in the following three chapters). Sandra, in the first of the original examples, started from an open position and developed hypotheses about her teaching by using classroom research procedures. Having identified a problem, Sandra then developed a plan for action. The open approach then is one where the teacher engages in classroom research as a reflective activity and derives from it a hypothesis that can be tested and provides a basis for action.

The closed approach deviates from the open in that many teachers have already identified a specific problem or hypothesis before engaging in classroom research. In this instance, their classroom research begins with the testing of an hypothesis. So with the example of Ann in chapter two, having heard about a new teaching method that applied to her subject area, she used classroom research to investigate the effectiveness of the approach.

The difference between open and closed reflects the derivation of the problem. In the first instance the hypothesis emerges as a result of critical reflection; in the second it is a given – it is extant, and the teacher having refined it, proceeds to testing. Both approaches reflect classroom research as it is defined in this book, because in both instances, the research is controlled by the teacher for the purpose of improving practice.

The contrast between open and closed problems can be represented in diagrammatic form as in Figure 5.1.

Type	Hypothesis
Open	Generating
Closed	Testing

FIGURE 5.1

Dillon (1983) has produced a similar (if rather more academic) schema for conceptualizing problem formation. He writes:

Three existential levels of problem and three corresponding psychological activities can be identified as forming part of those events which may be appropriately designated as problem finding. In existential terms, a problem can be existent, emergent or potential. An existent problem has fully-developed being and appearance in the phenomeno-logical field of events facing the observer. In psychological terms, the problem is evident and the observer perceives, recognizes, identifies it. At a second, less developed level an emergent problem exists which is implicit rather than evident. After probing the data – nosing about in the field of events, so to speak – the observer discovers or 'finds it'. At a still less developed level, a potential problem exists. No problem in an ontological sense exists qua problem, but constituent elements are present, striking the observer as an inchoate problem. By combining these and other elements in some way, the observer creates, produces or invents a problem. These descriptive terms relate the existential and psychological dimensions of problem find-ing activity at three levels, as follows: [see Figure 5.2]

My purpose of going into detail about problem forma-tion is simply to legitimize the position of teachers who want to get into classroom research just to find out about their teaching. Classroom research is not solely about exploring specific problems or testing explicit hypotheses. It is appropriate for teachers to use classroom research as a means of critically reflecting on their teaching and developing hypotheses about it.

Formulating Hypotheses

Whether or not teachers are initially involved in open or closed problems, they will have to formulate hypotheses at some stage.

As I suggested in chapter four, the teacher–researcher needs to clearly define his or her problem, for it is this definition that determines what data is collected and analysed. It is inevitable that our observations tend to be theory laden, so consequently it is important to formulate as explicitly as one can the hypotheses that are being tested. If, for example, a teacher is concerned about the problem of initiating classroom discussion, he or she may first hypothesize that asking more open-ended questions

PROBLEM LEVEL (existential/ psychological)	PROBLEM————	————ACTIVITY————	————SOLUTION
1. existing/evident	...as problematic	Perceiving the situation (RECOGNITION)	...as resolved
2. emergent/implicit	...for elements of a problem	Probing the data (DISCOVERY)	...for elements of a solution
3. potential/inchoate	...a defined problem	Producing the problem-event (INVENTION)	...a defined solution

FIGURE 5.2 *A conceptual scheme for comparing levels of problem finding and solving*

would encourage freer responses; a number of different hypotheses could be developed and tested around this contingency. The hypotheses, however, need to be extremely clear and precise. Because there are so many variables in the complex art of teaching, even a carefully worded hypothesis can sometimes only be reported as tentative and provisional. Pring (1978) gives some examples of classroom research hypotheses taken from the Ford Teaching project:

In order to cut out 'the guessing game' and move from a formal to an informal pattern, teachers may have to refrain from the following acts:

1. Changing Topic
Hypothesis. When teachers change the topic under discussion, they may prevent pupils from expressing and developing their own ideas, since pupils tend to interpret such interventions as attempts to get conformity to a particular line of reasoning.

2. Positive Reinforcers
Hypothesis. Utterances like 'good', 'interesting', 'right', in response to ideas expressed can prevent the expression and discussion of alternative ideas, since pupils tend to interpret them as attempts to legitimate the development of some ideas rather than others.

Following Popper's answer to the problem of induction (*vide* Magee 1973, Chap. 2), it is more appropriate to formulate hypotheses as unambiguously as we can, so as to expose them as clearly as possible to refutation. For as Popper pointed out, although empirical generalizations are in principle not verifiable they are falsifiable and, consequently, they can be tested by systematic attempts to refute them.

Theory and Theorizing

Now a word about theory. So far, I have used the word in two distinct senses. The first, refers to a set of personal assumptions, beliefs or presuppositions that individuals hold. Our view of the world, our individual construction of reality is at one level essentially theoretical. The second use of the word is in the more traditional or 'grand' sense, where theory refers to a coherent set of assumptions which purport to explain, predict and be used as a guide to practice. This is the sense in which the word was used when Ann, in the case study in chapter two, turned to theory in order to inform her classroom research problem.

Unfortunately, as I have hinted before and as has been clearly demonstrated by Pring (1978) and Stenhouse (1979), all too often educational theory in this second sense is not all that useful in telling us in a practical way how to behave in the classroom. In many instances, the gap between theory and practice is so large that it prevents any useful connection. This occurs because our theories are often not specific enough, or the propositions they contain are not easily generalized to individual situations. This, of course, is an unsatisfactory situation, and one that argues for a different approach to educational theory.

A viable alternative is to theorize about practice, and theorizing is a third way in which we can understand theory. Theorizing approaches theory through practice (the reverse of grand theory which goes from theory to practice), much in the same way as the hypotheses, assumptions and constructs we develop from classroom research procedures emerge from data gathered from actual classroom experiences. The discussion of grounded theory in chapter eight illustrates how theory can be generated from data gathered in a substantive situation. When we are engaged in classroom research we can be said to be engaged in educational theorizing because we are reflecting systematically and critically on practice. As Richard Pring (1978, 244–5) writes:

> Such systematic and critical examination will involve philosophizing, appealing to evidence, reference to ... theories. But there is no reason for saying that it will add up to a theory. (Classroom research is about) helping the practitioner to theorize i.e. think more systematically, critically and intelligently about his or her practice.

You will remember that Stenhouse (1975) in his discussion of the teacher–researcher illustrates this attitude when he suggested that the teacher, instead of accepting uncritically what a particular theory claims, implements it in the form of a working hypothesis or curriculum proposal. This thought captures two of the fundamental aspects of the autonomous professional teacher. First, they stand in control of knowledge rather than being subservient to it. Second, by doing this they are engaged in the process of theorizing and achieving self knowledge.

The idea of 'self knowledge' is an important one in this context. It refers to the individual internalization of ideas that empowers the person. It refers to those moments of clarity and power that occur when we understand a concept and see how we can use it in our personal or professional lives. It is an exciting and exhilarating moment and one which, for teachers and pupils alike, is too rare in our schools. This, as I understand it, is the basis of Polyani's (1962) writing on *Personal Knowledge*. Personal knowledge is that which is mediated through subjective experience and subsequently owned by the individual. Walt Whitman (1855) captures this thought in an evocative passage in *Leaves of Grass*:

> Stop this day and night with me and you shall possess the
>   origin of all poems,
> You shall possess the good of the earth and sun . . . . there
>   are millions of suns left,
> You shall no longer take things at second or third hand
> . . . .
>   nor look through the eyes of the dead . . . . nor feed on
>   the spectres in books,
> You shall not look through my eyes either, nor take things
>   from me,
> You shall listen to all sides and filter them from yourself.

There is now a burgeoning literature on praxis which is practical, critically reflective action and is similar to the term theorizing defined earlier. This is not the place to review this work, but it is important to mention it, as it reflects an extremely important theme in contemporary educational philosophy. Kemmis has recently written at length about praxis (Carr and Kemmis, 1983) and linked the idea to action research. It is appropriate then to conclude the chapter by quoting from Kemmis' (1983) article on action research:

> Practice, as it is understood by action researchers, is informed, committed action: praxis. Praxis has its roots in the commitment of the practitioner to wise and prudent action in a practical (concrete historical) situation. It is action which is informed by a 'practical theory', and which may, in its turn, inform and transform the theory which informed it. Practice is not to be understood as mere behaviour, but as strategic action undertaken with commitment in response to a present, immediate and problematic action context. Practical action is always risky; it requires wise judgement by the practitioner. As one theorist of practical action remarks, 'practical problems are problems about what to do ... their solution is only found in doing something'. In this sense the significance of practices can only be established in context: only under the 'compulsion' to act in a real historical situation can a commitment have force for the practitioner, on the one hand, and definite historical consequences for actors and the situation, on the other. Action is thus both a 'test' of commitment and the means by which practitioners can determine the adequacy of their understandings and of the situations in which practice occurs.
>
> Since only the practitioner has access to the commitments and practical theories which inform praxis, only the practitioner can study praxis. Action research, as the study of praxis, must thus be research into one's own practice. The action researcher will embark on a course of action strategically (deliberately experimenting with practice while aiming simultaneously for improvement in the practice, understanding of the practice and the situation in which the practice occurs); monitor the action, the circumstances under which it occurs and its consequences; and then retrospectively reconstruct an interpretation of the action in context as a basis for future action. Knowledge achieved in this way informs and refines both specific planning in relation to the practice being considered and the practitioner's general practical theory.

Commentary

In this chapter, I have discussed the formation of problems for classroom research by teachers. I have been at pains to point out that these problems can be either open or closed in so far as the teacher is engaged in hypothesis generation or testing. I have also pointed to some ways in which classroom research problems can be clarified and made more specific, and linked the whole discussion to a notion of theorizing, self knowledge and praxis. The underlying theme is that this is an important way for teachers to gain more control over their professional lives. Earlier in the chapter, I asked you to write down a list of topics for possible classroom research. Are you clearer now about the nature of the problem you wish to investigate? Do you understand how this process of understanding contributes to your professional judgement? How do you now view yourself in relation to knowledge and theory? In the next two chapters, we look very practically at the ways in which data for classroom research is collected by teachers.

Further Reading

For a discussion of hypothesis generation, it is useful to look at some of the Ford Teaching Project materials (e.g. Elliott, 1976). The article by Dillon (1983) on problem finding is very informative. Bryan Magee's (1973) monograph on Popper is a paragon of clarity and summarizes neatly Popper's solution to the problem of induction. Wilf Carr and Stephen Kemmis' (1983) book *Becoming Critical* contains a useful discussion on praxis and gives an introduction to the work of Habermas and critical theory. Finally, anyone interested in how praxis connects with social action and educational emancipation should read Paulo Freire's (1972) *Pedagogy of the Oppressed*.

6
Data Gathering

In this and the following chapter, I will discuss a variety
of techniques that teachers can use to gather information
about their teaching. This chapter is concerned with the
more open ended approaches and the following chapter
focuses on a variety of observation techniques. Although
the distinction between the two chapters is somewhat
arbitrary, it loosely reflects the open–closed distinction
drawn in the previous chapter.

I will observe a similar format in discussing each of the
approaches: the technique will be briefly described, advantages and disadvantages will be considered, appropriate uses will be stated and an example of the technique
in practice will be given. At the end of the chapter, I will
present a taxonomy of teacher research methods.

The Ford Teaching Project (Elliott & Adelman, 1976) in
general, and the booklet *Ways of Doing Research in One's
Own Classroom* (Bowen et al n.d.) in particular, provided
the inspiration for this chapter. The idea for the boxes
illustrating the advantages/disadvantages of the data collection methods came from the appendix to *Ways of Doing
Research in One's Own Classroom* and a number of the
points made there are reproduced here verbatim. Also, all
the methods of data collection mentioned below, with the
exception of sociometry, were used by the Ford Teaching
Project. Once again I am very grateful to the Ford
Teaching Project for allowing me to use their material in
this chapter.

Before describing these methods in more detail, two
caveats have to be entered. The first is that describing the
techniques individually may give a false impression of
orderliness and discreteness. In practice, these techniques

are more often than not used eclectically and in combination. Second, we need to remember the criteria established earlier which cautioned that the method employed should not be too demanding on the teacher's time.

Field Notes

Keeping field notes is a way of reporting observations, reflections, and reactions to classroom problems. Ideally, they should be written as soon as possible after a lesson, but can be based on impressionistic jottings made during a lesson. The greater the time-lapse between the event and recording it, the more difficult it becomes to reconstruct problems and responses accurately and retain conscious awareness of one's original thinking. Many teachers I know keep a notebook open on their desk or keep a space in their daybooks for jotting down notes as the lesson and the day progresses. Keeping a record in this way is not very time consuming and provides surprisingly frank information that is built up over time.

Field notes can be of a number of different types. They can be 'issue oriented' in so far as the observations focus on a particular aspect of one's teaching or classroom behaviour and constitute an ongoing record. On the other hand, they can reflect general impressions of the classroom, its climate or incidental events. Field notes can also be used to provide case study material of a particular child. This information should be descriptive rather than speculative so that a broad picture amenable to interpretation can be built up.

The main advantages and disadvantages of field notes are listed in point form in Box 6.1.

Three uses of field notes in classroom research are:

• they can focus on a particular issue or teaching behaviour over a period of time
• they can reflect general impressions of the classroom and its climate
• they can provide an ongoing description of an individual child that is amenable to interpretation and use in case study.

BOX 6.1

ADVANTAGES	DISADVANTAGES
•very simple to keep; no outsider needed	•need to fall back on aids such as question analysis sheets, tapes and transcripts for specific information
•provide good on-going record; used as a diary they give good continuity	•conversation impossible to record by field notes
•first hand information can be studied conveniently in teacher's own time	notebook works with small groups but not with a full class
•acts as an aide-memoire	•initially time-consuming
•helps to relate incidents, explore emerging trends	•can be highly subjective
•very useful if teacher intends to write a case study	

In this example Ian uses field notes to build up a picture of the work ethic in a low academic set of 12-13 year-olds.

I started making observations, keeping a note pad on the desk. I chose not to take a particular focus. After making initial observations on movement, posture, and seating arrangements, and after some interviews of a general nature concerning the pupils' attitudes to the teaching of language and the organization into sets that the pupils had to submit to, a picture of the work ethic of a low academic set was gradually built up.

For each distinct activity that goes on in the English language lesson (language laboratory work, story writing, grammar skills, etc.) the working environments and climates are different. In language work for example, there is always an initial rush to complete *one* card – the minimum requirement. When this is completed, although another card is often collected, intensive work ceases and chatting about the weekend, with some desultory work, is the norm (the lesson is first period Monday). This ritualized behaviour has the function of reaffirming certain social groups, and talk is, interestingly enough, voluntarily kept to a quite quiet level. The various friendship groups have distinct topics of conversation which don't vary much over the year. Changes to the seating, which I have tried, cause a much higher level of noise. All the other English activities – each one has one lesson a week – have different structures and patterns of social interaction, attitudes, and noise levels which have built up over time.

I noted that the pattern of work throughout the term – and the year – is affected by traditional school rituals. The arrangement of pupils into sets is reviewed at the end of each term and this ritual always influences work rate and conversation:

Girl: You 'eard about moving up yet, sir?
Teacher: No, I've been asked to make three recommend-ations to go up and down. Mr ... will make the decision. (Chorus of inquiries)
Girl: Shut up you – you're thick. If you move, it'll be down. I hope I move up – we do no work in 'ere. 'Alf of 'em can't even write (looking at the boys). (Cheers from boys)

The low status of the set is always a factor in the pupils' perceptions of their ability and in their attitude to work.

[This example is taken from a series of teacher–researcher reports on children's thinking (in Hull *et al*, 1985).]

Audio Tape Recording

Audio tape recording is one of the most popular teacher research methods. Transcripts are excellent for those situations where teachers require a very specific and accurate record of a limited aspect of their teaching, or of a particular interaction, say between a specific teacher and child or between two children. Also, simply playing back tapes of one's teaching can be very illuminating and provide useful starting points for further investigation. Having a tape deck in one's car is a great asset for doing this.

Playing back tapes or making transcripts can be very

time consuming and expensive, however, unless the
method is used judiciously. The Ford Teaching Project
teachers and staff were very enthusiastic about this
method, but they did have secretarial support for making
transcripts. Most teachers do not, and for that reason, I
advise against it as a broad spectrum diagnostic tool.

On the practical side, the use of the tape recorder
requires some technical knowledge so make certain you
can use it before taking it into class. It is important when
recording to ensure that the microphone is picking up
what is intended, and this also may require practice.
Pupils often find the presence of a tape recorder in the
class disturbing and have to be introduced to the technique over time. Always check with pupils and other
teachers or adults that they do not mind you recording the
conversation or discussion.

The main advantages and disadvantages of the audio
tape recorder are listed in point form in Box 6.2.

BOX 6.2

ADVANTAGES	DISADVANTAGES
•very successfully monitors all conversations within range of the recorder	•nothing visual – does not record silent activities
•provides ample material with great ease	•transcription largely pro-hibitive because of expense and time involved
•versatility – can be transported or left with a group	•masses of material may provide little relevant information
•records personality developments	•can disturb pupils because of its novelty; can be inhibiting
•can trace development of a group's activities	•continuity can be disturbed by the practical problems of operating

Two uses of the tape recorder in classroom research are:

- as a general diagnostic tool for identifying aspects of one's teaching
- for providing detailed evidence on specific aspects of teaching through the use of transcripts.

In this example Val uses an audio tape recorder as an aid to understanding children's thinking in relation to sketch maps in geography.

The class (of very bright eleven year olds) was arranged in groups of four or five pupils and each group was given copies of the four maps and asked to discuss them and decide which they thought was 'best'. I only had access to one tape recorder and was only able therefore to record one discussion. When I listened to the tape I realized that discussion clearly had potential as a research tool and that this strategy for gaining access to pupils' critical thinking was worth repeating. Pupils were realistic in their criticisms and were to some extent impersonal. The discussion helped me to see what criteria they were using and how the range of their considerations might be extended.

In my next attempt . . . (there was only one tape-recorder available), there were several groups responding to the maps, so each group chose a leader and he or she gave a report to the class at the end of the discussion and it was the final reports that were taped. Some of the spontaneity of the original discussion was lost but nevertheless some interesting points emerged.

It seemed that the brighter pupils were more methodical and precise in their criticism:

> *Simon*: Our verdict on map 1 was that a ruler could have been used and some of the buildings had doors missing and that there wasn't any scale . . . title, key or north direction.
> Map 3 – it's a drawing, it's not a map.
> Map 4 – that's quite good, that's more of a map, they have got a key and direction and a suitable title.
> *Sarah*: We thought map 1 wasn't very good because the writing is too small.
> Map 3 wasn't very good – too artistic.
> *Valerie*: Map 2 was the best because it showed all the roads and railways and bridges.

[This example is taken from a series of teacher–researcher reports on children's thinking (in Hull *et al*, 1985).]

Pupil Diaries

It is common practice in many schools for pupils to keep a daily log. This is also a quick way of obtaining information, as teachers normally check pupil diaries as a matter of course. Also, pupil diaries provide an interesting contrast to the field notes kept by the teacher on the same topic. Once the pupils have been taken into the teacher's confidence and are aware of the teacher's concern to research his or her teaching then these diaries are an excellent way of obtaining honest feedback, particularly when the pupils retain the right to decide whether the teacher has access to the diary. The teacher can use pupil diaries as feedback on a particular teaching episode, or to gain an indication of the general class climate, or to assess the progress of an individual pupil.

The main advantages and disadvantages of pupil diaries are listed in point form in Box 6.3.

Three uses of pupil diaries in classroom research are:

• they provide a pupil perspective on a teaching episode
• they provide data on the general climate of the classroom
• they provide information for triangulation.

In this example Judy is using pupil diaries as part of her strategy for reorganizing her maths class.

I used the diaries mainly as immediate feedback for myself and as an aid in monitoring the daily progress of the students. Following are samples of information that I gathered from the various student diaries during a four week period:

1. there were explanations as to why they hadn't completed a number of assignments for my substitute while I was at a convention
2. throughout the four weeks the students used the logs to

BOX 6.3

ADVANTAGES	DISADVANTAGES
•provides feedback from pupil's perspective	•may not be an established practice in the school
•can be either focused on a specific teaching episode or related to the general classroom climate	•difficult for younger children to record their thoughts and feelings
•can be part of a lesson	•pupils may be inhibited in discussing their feelings with the teacher
•can help in identifying individual pupil problems	•pupil's accounts are obviously subjective
•involves pupil in improving the quality of the class	
•provides a basis for triangulation	

   tell me when they were having trouble with an assignment and to ask to see me the next day for help
3. a number of students suggested that I put in a center
   containing mazes and logic puzzles that they could go to
   when they had completed all their assignments
4. occasionally, a pupil would ask me to change their
   seating arrangement as they weren't able to work near a
   certain person
5. many of them began to use the log to establish a private
   conversation between us
6. I used the logs to indicate when I was disappointed in a
   student's performance or behavior and to question them
   about it. I found that they were more open since they
   weren't put on the spot in front of their classmates
7. some of them mentioned when they felt I had let the
   noise level get too high or when they had been able to
   do more than usual because it had been exceptionally
   quiet
8. they pointed out when they had wasted time waiting for
   me to get their books marked so they could finish off
   their corrections

9. I found it especially helped me monitor the progress of
   my less assertive students
10. the students would indicate when they felt I had given
    too heavy a work load for the week
11. students twice pointed out that they had come to me for
    assistance and I had been too busy to help them.

I felt that these logs were one of the most valuable aspects
of my research project. They weren't always relevant to my
actual research, but the personal contact I managed to
establish with each of my students was of more importance
to me than keeping them on target concerning their work
in the math program.

Interviews

Interviewing in classroom research can take four forms: it
can occur between teacher/pupil, observer/pupil, pupil/
pupil and occasionally teacher/observer. This latter
activity, however, normally occurs as a consequence of
peer observation (see chapter seven). Because teacher/
pupil interviews are very time consuming, it may be more
profitable to devote that time to general classroom
meetings, and only talk individually with pupils (for
research purposes) when a specific instance warrants it.
On the other hand, individual interviews are often very
productive sources of information for a participant
observer who wants to verify observations he or she has
previously made. Pupil–pupil interviews can provide rich
sources of data, particularly if the pupil interviewer keeps
to an interview schedule prepared by the teacher. It is
good idea to tape record these individual interviews for
future reference, particularly if the encounters are relatively short.

Walker and Adelman (1975, 140) make a number of
points about effective interviewing:

1. be a sympathetic, interested and attentive listener,
   without taking an active conservative role; this is a
   way of conveying that you value and appreciate the
   child's opinion
2. be neutral with respect to subject matter. Do not
   express your own opinions either on the subjects

being discussed by the children or on the children's ideas about these subjects, and be especially careful not to betray feelings of surprise or disapproval at what the child knows
3. your own sense of ease is also important. If you feel hesitant or hurried, the students will sense this feeling and behave accordingly
4. the students may also be fearful that they will expose an attitude or idea that you don't think is correct. Reassure along the lines of 'Your opinions are important to me. All I want to know is what you think – this isn't a test and there isn't any one answer to the questions I want to ask'
5. specifically we suggest that you:
   • phrase questions similarly each time
   • keep the outline of interview questions before you
   • be prepared to reword a question if it is not understood or if the answer is vague and too general. Sometimes it is hard not to give an 'answer' to the question in the process of rewording it.

The main advantages and disadvantages of interviewing are listed in point form in Box 6.4 i, ii and iii.

Three uses of the interview in classroom research are:

• to focus on a specific aspect of teaching or classroom life in detail
• teacher/pupil classroom discussion can provide general diagnostic information
• to improve classroom climate.

In this example, Marianne asks a colleague to interview the 'problem' pupil who is the focus of her research project.

I wanted to know Shane's feelings and his attitude towards me, his teacher, and whether he felt I was 'picking on him', etc.. I asked Miss Ledinski to interview him personally so he would not feel intimidated by me. Miss Ledinski agreed, and I was surprised by the positive com-

BOX 6.4 i

Teacher/pupil

ADVANTAGES	DISADVANTAGES
•teacher in direct contact with pupil	•time consuming
•pupil familiar with teacher, therefore more at ease	•may be carried out with some form of recording equipment, with attendant disadvantages
•teacher able to seek information s/he wants directly and not through a ream of irrelevant information	•frequently difficult to get younger children to explain their thoughts and feelings
•can be done in lesson time or outside the class	
•can follow up problems immediately when they arise and get information while minds are still fresh	

ments he gave about me:

Q. What do you think of Miss Schmidt?
A. • a good teacher
   • she does nice work for us – stories, and that

Q. How does she treat you?
A. • okay, except one day she wouldn't let me use the phone – that wasn't fair because it was important

Q. Is she fair to you?
A. • sometimes she says I do bad things, and I don't

Q. How would you like to change her?
A. • not to yell.
   • not nag.
   • if she didn't do this, she would be perfect!

BOX 6.4 ii

Observer/Pupil

ADVANTAGES	DISADVANTAGES
•leaves teacher free as the interviewer discovers initial information from the pupil	•pupil unfamiliar with observer may be reluctant to divulge relevant information
•pupil frequently more candid with the outsider than with class teacher or teacher from within the school	•mutual uncertainty
•outsider is likely to be more objective	•if the teacher is the primary agent in the research, then s/he will get his information second hand and subject to the biases of the interviewer
•outsider can focus information the child provides along predetermined lines of investigation	•the whole set up is time consuming as information goes from pupil to interviewer to teacher
	•difficult to obtain a skilled outsider

BOX 6.4 iii

Pupil/Pupil

ADVANTAGES	DISADVANTAGES
•pupils may be more candid with each other	•pupils may find the activity too unfamiliar
•leaves teacher free	•may encourage disruption
•can occur during lesson time	•has to be recorded and played to teacher
•may produce unanticipated/unusual perspectives	

Q. What kinds of things does she say to you in a day?
A. • you do good work
    • she sends me to see Mr. Day if my work is good
    • Get to work, get to work!

In teaching during the next periods, I tried to reinforce Shane with positive comments and involve him in the group as a whole rather than singling him out.

Video Tape Recorder

The video tape recorder is increasingly being used by teachers as a means of gathering general information about their teaching. It allows the teacher to observe many facets of his or her teaching quickly, and provides heuristic and accurate information for diagnosis. After this, the teacher may wish to use a different method to examine specific aspects of his or her teaching.

Many of the teacher–researchers I know use the video on an intermittent but regular basis to enable them to keep in touch with their teaching. If an observer or student can be used to operate the video recorder, then more attention can be paid to specific teaching episodes (identified beforehand) or the reaction of particular students.

Two concerns related to the video tape recorder are cost and its disruptive influence (because of its novelty) on classroom behaviour patterns. The first objection, cost, is slowly being overcome. Increasingly, many schools have a video recorder at their disposal, and because few teachers actually research their teaching, video machines are often available. Second, the novelty value of the equipment rapidly disappears with use. I advise teachers to introduce the equipment to the pupils first, demonstrate how it works and then leave it standing in the classroom for some time before actually taping. This allows both pupils and teachers to become accustomed to its presence. Another tip is to keep the monitor switched off except during demonstration sessions.

The main advantages/disadvantages of the video tape recorder are listed in point form in Box 6.5.

BOX 6.5

ADVANTAGES	DISADVANTAGES
•enables all situations to be constantly reviewed	•expensive to obtain
•origin of problems can be diagnosed	•can be very conspicuous and distracting
•behavioural patterns of teacher and pupil can be seen	•if camera is directed by operator it will only record that which s/he deems to be of importance; operator acts as editor
•patterns of progress over long periods can be clearly charted	

Three uses of video recorders in classroom research are:

•in obtaining visual material of the total teaching situation
•in acting as an aid to diagnosis
•as a means of examining in detail a specific teaching episode.

In this example I describe the first experience Geoff, a student on one of my inservice courses, had with the video tape recorder.

Geoff is a deputy head teacher in a special school. His pupils are severely impaired, but the expectation is that they will eventually be able to cope by themselves in some limited way. To give his pupils that basic level of life-skill is Geoff's main goal. Geoff used the video to examine his teaching and to try and find an answer to the question 'why is everything so time consuming'.

Geoff decided to video the morning session from 9:30 to 10:15 which was the most structured and high energy time of the day. During the lesson the nursery nurse was also involved in the class. Before videoing, Geoff identified a series of topics that he wanted to get information on:

- maximum time worked by each pupil
- time wasted by each pupil
- time unavoidably lost
- time be spent with each pupil
- number of tasks accomplished in the 45 minute session by each pupil.

The video taping session went well. Geoff had had the camera in his room for a few days so the pupils were used to having it around. With a wide angle lens he was able to capture all the activity in the class. Geoff then began reviewing the tape. Besides gathering data on the points above he also detailed the following:

- amount of time he spent out of the class on administrative duties
- the number of times he praised/reprimanded a pupil
- how long the pupils were left unsupervised
- time spent by nursery nurse with each pupil
- pupil's reaction to attention.

Geoff then analysed the tape for each pupil and produced a detailed analysis of how individual lessons were spent. From this information Geoff was able to derive a number of hypotheses concerning the class and set up a programme for utilizing the time more effectively.

Questionnaires

Questionnaires that ask specific questions about aspects of the classroom, curriculum, or teaching method are a quick and simple way of obtaining broad and rich information from pupils. It is important, however, particularly in the primary grades, to be relatively unsophisticated in the structuring of the questions. Condense the usual five point scale to two or three responses, keep the questions simple, and use the basic 'what did you like best', 'what did you like least', 'what would you do differently' type of open ended question.

With younger (and older) pupils it is often more profitable to use a happy face as the criterion response to

Inquiry/Discover follow-up questionnaire

Please put a ring round the answer you wish to give to each question. If you are not sure ring the nearest to what you think.

1. How much of the lesson did you enjoy? — All of it/Some of it/None

2. How much do you think you learnt? — Nothing/Something/A lot

3. How much did you understand? — Most of it/Some of it/Nothing

4. Could you find the books, information, equipment you needed? — None/Some of it/Most of it

5. Did other people help you? — A lot/A little/Not at all

6. Did other people stop you working? — A Lot/Sometimes/Not at all

7. Did the teacher help you — Enough/Not enough

8. Did the lesson last — Long enough/Too long/Not long enough

9. Was the lesson — Boring/Interesting

10. Did you need anything you could not find? — Yes/No

11. Where did you get help from? — Teacher/Group/Someone else

12. Did you find this work — Easy/Hard/Just about right

13. Write down anything which made it hard for you to learn.

14. Write down anything you particularly enjoyed about this lesson

[Questionnaire designed by Roger Pols in Bowen *et al* (n.d): reprinted with permission.]

FIGURE 6.1 *A Sample questionnaire*

FIGURE 6.2

questions as in Figure 6.2. More imaginatively cartoon pictures can be used, as in Figure 6.3: the possibilities are endless!

The main advantages and disadvantages of the questionnaire are listed in point form in Box. 6.6

The main use of the questionnaire in classroom research is to obtain quantitative responses to specific predetermined questions.

Examples of questionnaires are given in Figures 6.1 and 6.3.

BOX 6.6

ADVANTAGES	DISADVANTAGES
•easy to administer; quick to fill in • easy to follow up	•analysis is time consuming •extensive preparation to get clear and relevant questions • difficult to get questions that explore in depth
•provides direct comparision of groups and individuals	•effectiveness depends very much on reading ability and comprehension of the child

•provides feedback on:
    attitudes
    adequacy of resources
    adequacy of teacher help
    preparation for next session
    conclusions at end of term
•data is quantifiable
	•children may be fearful of answering candidly
	
	•children will try to produce 'right' answers

NAME _____   ROOM _____   TEACHER _____

1.   How do you feel when your teacher reads a story aloud?

2.   How do you feel when someone gives you a book for a present?

3.   How do you feel about reading books for fun at home?

4.   How do you feel when you are asked to read aloud to your group?

5.   How do you feel when you are asked to read aloud to your teacher?

FIGURE 6.3   *Reading attitude survey*

Sociometry

Sociometric analysis or sociometry is a technique used to measure the emotional structure of a group. As a diagnostic instrument, sociometry's purpose is to highlight the feelings of attraction, indifference and rejection that occur within a group and between its members. The approach has obvious applications to classrooms where teachers want to discover the social structure of the class for research and other purposes. The most important 'other purpose' is to identify pupils who are socially isolated in order to take remedial action.

Before administering a sociometric test, it is important to ensure that the pupils know each other fairly well, that confidentiality is established, and that action be taken as a consequence. Sociometry in this sense is a dynamic process that can lead to improvement in children's attitudes and relationships and the general enhancement of a classroom climate.

Congdon (1978, 6) describes a method for administering the sociometric test:

> Each child is handed a slip of blank paper and told to write his name at the top. Some teachers prefer to have the names of all pupils in the class written on the blackboard. It is always advisable to write up the names of any pupils who are absent. The test should be meaningful to the pupils. So, for example, the context of the test could be a project. After deciding on a project the pupils could be told that they will be allowed to work in groups and that the groups would be made up according to their own choices.
>
> On the left hand side of the sheet the pupils are asked to write the name of the person with whom they would most like to work in a group. Underneath they are asked to write the name of the one they would like next best, then the next and so on. They can be told to write as many names as they wish or none at all. The pupil is then asked to turn over the sheet and again down the left hand side of the page to write the names of any children with whom they do not wish to work. The teacher again tells them that they may write as many names as they wish or none at all. And what is more important she tells them that the names will be only known to herself i.e. the choices are made privately and no pupil should be told either who chose him or how

many choices he received. In this way on one's feelings are hurt.

After the test has been administered, the pupil choices are analysed to establish the structure of relationships within the class. The best known and easiest understood method of doing this is the sociogram. Congdon (1978, 7) continues to describe how a sociogram is constructed:

> In drawing a sociogram it is often useful to begin with the most chosen pupil and add the symbols for any pupils who reciprocate his or her choices. Next, pupils who have mutual choices with this group can be added. When these have been exhausted then a fresh group can be drawn up starting with the next most highly-chosen pupil and so on. The sociogram can be completed by filling in the unreciprocated choices.

Figure 6.4 is an example of a sociogram for a group of eight individuals with the symbols most commonly used marked on it.

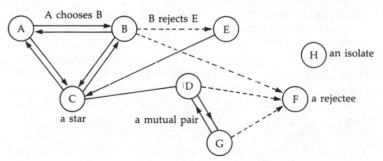

FIGURE 6.4 *Example of a sociogram*

Clearly in Figure 6.4 pupils E, F and H are unpopular and this information encourages the teacher to act to remedy this situation; action that can also be monitored through other classroom research techniques. The sociogram is a useful method for teacher–researchers who wish to explore the social structure of their class and the relationship between pupils. It also provides a starting point for action and further research.

The major advantages and disadvantages of sociometry are listed in point form in Box 6.7.

BOX 6.7

ADVANTAGES	DISADVANTAGES
•simple way to discover social relationships in class	•possibility of compounding the isolation of some
	•pupils
•provides guide to action	
•can be integrated into class activity	

The main use of sociometry in classroom research is to disclose the social structure of the class.

In this example Ann was using a behaviour modification 'game' to improve the level of assignment completion in her maths class.

Since I had scruples about such a game causing social rejection of the target pupils, a sociogram was done before and after the experiment. Pupils were each asked to name three children they would like to sit next to during art lessons or storytime. It was stressed that this would be a non-academic, non-competitive time. The first choices were assigned three points, the second two points and the third one point. Points were totaled and the results entered on a graph.

Pre and post use of the sociogram showed that the popularity of the target pupils was not detrimentally affected by the game. None of them were social isolates but they all fell into the lower half of the class.

Documentary Evidence

Documents (memos, letters, position papers, examination papers, newspaper clippings, etc.) surrounding a curriculum or other educational concern can illuminate rationale and purpose in interesting ways. The use of such material can provide background information and understanding of issues that would not otherwise be available.

BOX 6.8

ADVANTAGES	DISADVANTAGES
•illuminate issues surrounding a curriculum or teaching method	•obtaining documents can be time consuming
•provide context, background and understanding	•certain documents may be difficult to obtain
•provide an easy way of obtaining other people's perceptions	•certain persons may be unwilling to share 'confidential' documents

The main advantages and disadvantages of documentary evidence are listed in point form in Box 6.8.

The main use of documents in classroom research is that they provide a context for understanding a particular curriculum or teaching method.

In this example Gill used documents to understand the nature of the art curriculum.

During her work for a postgraduate degree Gill, an art teacher, examined some of the influences on the art curriculum. Her reason for doing this was largely personal: increasingly she was feeling a tension between her aspirations for art teaching and the general approach to the art curriculum that she was being encouraged to adopt. Gill's approach to the teaching of art was essentially child centred. She has a commitment to developing a pupil's artistic talents and her teaching style and the activities she set her pupils were designed to achieve this goal. Her investigation involved examining a range of past papers and examiners comments. To her chagrin she found that the art curriculum in general was influenced not by pupil achievement or aspirations but more by the examiners' (rather traditional) comments. This discovery served at least to explain her tension. It also encouraged her to develop a scheme of work in painting for younger pupils and propose alternative syllabi for examination pupils that integrated her own ideas on art teaching with the more traditional approach.

Slide/Tape Photography

Photographs and slides, with or without audio tape commentary, are a useful way of recording critical incidents in classrooms or of illustrating particular teaching episodes. They can also be used to support other forms of data gathering (e.g. interviews or field notes) or as a means for providing reference points for interviews or discussions. This approach is increasingly being superceded by video.

The main advantages and disadvantages of slide/tape photography are listed in point form in Box 6.9.

The main use of photographic slides in classroom research is as a means of illustrating critical incidents, and of provoking discussion.

Rob Walker and Clem Adelman's (1975) *A Guide to Classroom Observation* contains advice on and examples of the use of photography in classroom research.

BOX 6.9

ADVANTAGES	DISADVANTAGES
•advantage may be obtained by looking at photographs of kids working, or at end products of their work, and as a stimulus for discussion	•shows isolated situations; difficulty of being in the right place at the right time; concentrates on small groups and individuals; not classes; records nothing in depth
•as an instrument which helps you get observation and comment from other teachers who were not present at the time	•slides may not truly depict activities of the children, if photographer is selective
	•can be a great distraction
	•shows nothing oral
	•film processing time can result in lengthy period between session being recorded and feedback requires photographer

Case Study

The case study is a relatively formal analysis of an aspect of classroom life. One way of producing a teacher research case study is described in the first section of chapter nine (see Figure 9.1). Helen Simon's (1980) *Towards a Science of the Singular* contains more detailed advice on producing educational case studies. Some teachers may wish to produce case studies for a university course they are taking or as research towards a higher degree. These situations apart, it is unlikely that teachers will devote time to producing a formal case report of their teacher–researcher efforts every time they undertake a project.

The main advantages and disadvantages of the case study are listed in point form in Box 6.10.

The main use of the case study in classroom research is that it provides a relatively formal and fairly definitive analysis of a specific aspect of teaching behaviour or classroom life.

Examples of teacher research case studies are given in chapter two.

BOX 6.10

ADVANTAGES	DISADVANTAGES
•a relatively simple way of plotting the progress of a course or a pupil's or group's reaction to teaching methods	•in order for the case study to be of value it must be fairly exhaustive; this means that it will be time consuming in its preparation and its writing
•information yielded by case studies will tend to give a more accurate and representative picture than will any one of the research methods detailed above; case studies draw on data gathered by many methods	•feedback available to teacher only after considerable lapse of time

Technique	Advantages(s)	Disadvantage(s)	Use(s)
Field Notes	simple; on going; personal; aide memoire	subjective; needs practice	• specific issue • case study • general impression
Audio Tape Recording	versatile; accurate; provides ample data	transcription difficult; time consuming; often inhibiting	• detailed evidence • diagnostic
Pupil Diaries	provides pupils perspective	subjective	• diagnostic • triangulation
Interviews and Discussions	can be teacher–pupil, observer–pupil, pupil–pupil	time consuming	• specific in depth information
Video Tape Recorder	visual and comprehensive	awkward and expensive; can be distracting	• visual material • diagnostic

Questionnaires	highly specific; easy to administer; comparative	time consuming to analyse; problem of 'right' answers	• specific information & feedback
Sociometry	easy to administer; provides guide to action	can threaten isolated pupils	• analyses social relationships
Documentary evidence	illuminative	difficult to obtain; time consuming	• provides context & information
Slide/Tape Photography	illuminative; promotes discussion	difficult to obtain; superficial	• illustrates critical incidents
Case Study	accurate; representative; uses range of techniques	time consuming	• comprehensive overview of an issue • publishable format

FIGURE 6.5 *Taxonomy of classroom research techniques*

Commentary

In this chapter, I have described a variety of ways in which
data can be gathered for the purpose of classroom
research. The techniques described in this chapter are
basically open ended in so far as they are used most
effectively for diagnostic purposes. Although I have
described these techniques individually, it is important to
realize that they can and are most often used eclectically
and in combination. But each has a specific purpose and
is best suited to a particular situation. A taxonomy of the
main advantages, disadvantages and uses of the various
techniques is given in Figure 6.5.

Further Reading

Additional information about the techniques of classroom
research can be found in the publications associated with
the Ford Teaching Project (see Appendix A). Elliott and
Adelman's (1976) case study of the Ford Teaching Project
in the Open University curriculum course *Innovation at the
Classroom Level* is informative and useful, as is the Ford
Teaching Project booklet *Ways of Doing Research in One's
Own Classroom* (Bowen *et al* n.d). Walker and Adelman's
(1975) book *A Guide to Classroom Observation* contains much
practical advice. An American book on clinical supervision
(Acheson and Gall, 1980) also provides information on
many of the techniques described in this chapter.

7

Observation in Classroom Research

In this chapter, I consider a series of data gathering techniques that utilize observation as their modus operandi. In the previous chapter, I outlined ten relatively open-ended methods of gathering data that are generally diagnostic and controlled by the teacher. The approaches described in this chapter are more structured, require more external help, and are more suited to the testing of hypotheses and to the closed type of problems discussed in chapter five. The four approaches to observation described in this chapter are peer observation, clinical supervision, structured observation and interaction schedules. The sections on peer observation and clinical supervision outline different approaches to classroom observation and those on structured observation and interaction schedules discuss more specific techniques.

Peer Observation

Peer observation refers to the observation of one's teaching by another (usually a friendly colleague). Sometimes called participant observation, this method provides the teacher–researcher with a flexible source of data and also a means of support. I try to encourage teachers to engage in classroom research in pairs or small groups for a number of reasons. Among them is the emotional support they gain from each other, particularly as this activity is initially threatening. It is now fairly well established that teachers learn best from other teachers, and take criticism most easily from this source. It is ideal if teachers in peer groups can act as observers for each other, and this mutual exchange of roles quickly breaks down barriers which would be monolithic to outside researchers.

The participant observer can also play any number of differing roles. They can observe a lesson in general, focus on specific aspects of the teaching and talk to pupils all during one observation period. This lightens the teacher's problem of analysis and tends to increase the objectivity of the data gathered. In addition, the observer may also be able to note incidents that the teacher would ordinarily miss.

The major advantages of peer observation are that it lightens the teacher's problem of analysis and ensures, through the use of an observer, more unbiased and objective data gathering. Although it may sometimes be difficult to obtain the services of an observer, their ability to be flexible and to focus on a wide variety of teaching situations outweighs that disadvantage.

In this extended example, Heather Lockhart describes how she went about observing her colleague Maureen's teaching.

Maureen has recently begun to doubt the effectiveness of her questioning techniques. She asked me to observe a review lesson on a 'Plants and Seeds' unit she had recently completed. We decided to concentrate on observing the effectiveness of her questioning techniques rather than the lesson content.

We also decided that I would be in the classroom strictly as an observer. I would not participate in the lesson in any way. We felt that, as many of the children in the room had been former students of mine and because I work with her class two periods every week, the children were familiar with me and comfortable in my presence. We also decided not to use a tape recorder or video tape so that the children would not be inhibited by them. Maureen and I discussed the most effective way of monitoring and decided on a checklist. I made a checklist and showed it to Maureen. Maureen agreed that it should give us the information we needed.

I positioned myself in the room within the children's immediate sight but slightly separated from the group. As I was within the field of their vision, I would not be causing distraction through children turning to check to see what I was doing. By separating myself slightly from the group, I was implying that I was not participating in the lesson. Maureen reinforced this by telling the children that I was going to watch because I didn't believe that they knew anything about plants and seeds. As we had predicted, outside of an occasional quick glance or smile, the children tended to ignore my presence.

When we first sat down, Maureen allowed the class about a minute of 'wiggle time' before she began to speak. She quickly explained my presence, then went directly into the lesson. She began by giving the children 'fact' questions that they could answer directly from the pictures. The responses were slow to come. Few children volunteered to answer the first few questions. As Maureen continued with the 'fact' questions, the children became more excited and eager to answer.

Maureen then began to inject 'inference questions'. The children were experiencing such success with 'fact questions' that they experienced no trouble in making inferences from the pictures. She then interspersed questions which required the children to form opinions. Again, the children responded freely and confidently. The children began to get restless after about fifteen minutes and their attention began to wander. Maureen realized what was happening and quickly ended the lesson.

Looking at the checklist after the observation, my reactions to Maureen's questioning techniques were confirmed. The questions were asked clearly and concisely. The children had full understanding of the type of response that was being elicited. As they understood the questions, they were comfortable and eager to respond.

Maureen's interaction with the children was warm and caring. She listened carefully and respectfully to each response whether the response was incorrect or correct. She encouraged hesitant children by smiling at them, giving verbal encouragement or nodding while the child was speaking. She was careful to ensure that each child had the opportunity to respond at least once during the lesson.

I feel that Maureen has excellent questioning techniques. This includes the variety in the type of questions she asks, the manner in which she uses her voice, the positive reinforcement she employs, the pace of the lesson and the warmth she shows towards the children.

I feel that Maureen's main problem with questioning techniques is that she doesn't recognize her expertise in this area. I would suggest she tape the lessons that use intensive questioning methods and analyse the results for her own benefit.

Clinical Supervision

Clinical supervision is a technique that has enjoyed much popularity in North America, where it was developed as a method of supervising student teachers, but it is also suited for use in classroom research situations. It is a more structured form of peer observation that focuses on a teacher's instructional performance utilizing a three phase approach to the observation of teaching events.

The three essential phases of the clinical supervision process are a planning conference, classroom observation, and a feedback conference. The planning conference provides the observer and teacher with an opportunity to reflect on the proposed lesson, and this leads to a mutual decision to collect observational data on an aspect of the teacher's teaching. During the classroom observation phase, the observer observes the teacher teach and collects objective data on that aspect of teaching they agreed upon earlier. It is in the feedback conference that the observer and teacher share the information, decide on remedial action (if necessary), and often plan to collect further observational data. Variations on this process depicted in Figure 7.1 are suggested by different writers on the topic, but all follow the same basic pattern. It is important, however, to realize that to be effective all three phases of the process need to be gone through systematically.

There are a number of principles that are important to consider in clinical supervision. First, the climate of interaction between teacher and observer needs to be non-threatening, helping and one of mutual trust. Second, the focus of the activity should be on improving instruction and the reinforcing of successful patterns, rather than on criticism of unsuccessful patterns, or changing the teacher's personality. Third, the process depends on the

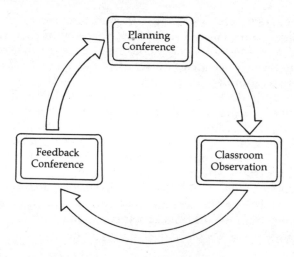

FIGURE 7.1 *The supervision cycle*

collection and use of objective observational data, not unsubstantiated value judgements. Fourth, teachers are encouraged to make inferences about their teaching from the data, and to use the data to construct hypotheses that can be tested out in the future. Fifth, each cycle of supervision is part of an ongoing process that builds on the other. Sixth, both observer and teacher are engaged in mutual interaction that can lead to improvement in teaching and observational skills for both.

An example of clinical supervision is given by Marsha and George who worked together in the same school.

Marsha had already observed several of George's Grade 8 social studies classes. During a planning conference, they went over George's lesson plan on current events. George identified his objectives, one of which was to involve as many pupils as possible in discussing a particular news story. They decided to focus the observation on the type of questions George asked, and the pupils' responses. Marsha suggested she use a seating plan on which to 'tally' the voluntary and solicited comments from the pupils. George agreed and also requested that she jot down his questions verbatim.

During the lesson, Marsha recorded information for the twenty minutes George had planned for the discussion. Afterwards, as they went over the data, patterns began to emerge. George noticed that, although the discussion had been lively, only twelve out of the twenty-eight pupils had participated (he had thought during the lesson that more were involved). Also certain types of questions tended to elicit more complete responses.

They both decided that it might be useful if George sequenced his questions from factual types (to establish a common knowledge base) to more open-ended, opinion questions. Also, now that he knew which pupils were reticent, George would attempt to involve them more in class discussions. Marsha suggested a couple of techniques that worked for her, and George was excited about trying them out. The feedback conference ended with both agreeing to use the same observation focus in the near future to compare the results of George's new strategies.

Structured Observation

In the previous sections, I discussed two approaches to classroom observation, one that was *ad hoc* and informal and the other where the process was structured. What was not discussed in these sections was how the observer gathered information about the other's teaching. In this and the following section I want to look at two ways of doing that. Below, I discuss simple observation checklists that are tailored by the teacher to fit a particular situation. In the following section, I deal with more specific inter-action scales.

When teachers observe each other teaching, all they often require are simple ways of gathering information on basic topics, such as questioning techniques, on-task and off-task behaviours and classroom management. It is usually preferable for teachers to devise their own obser-vation schedules, to 'invent' them for a particular pur-pose. By doing this, the teacher develops more ownership over the investigation and there is probably a better 'fit' between the object of the observation and the data gather-ing method.

Before devising the observation checklist, it is useful to ask some organizing questions in order to ascertain the purpose of the observation. These questions are illustrative:

1. What is the purpose of the observation?
2. What teacher behaviours are worth observing?
3. What is focus of the observation?
4. What data gathering methods will best serve the purpose?
5. How will the data be used?

The next step is to devise the observation schedule. What follows are some examples of observation schedules developed by teachers who were concerned with gathering data on questioning techniques and on/off task behaviours. Other illustrations of teacher devised checklists are found in the examples and case studies cited throughout the book.

Observing questioning techniques

1. Question distribution: in Box 7.1 the circles represent pupils, when they answer a question the number of

BOX 7.1

the question is entered in to their circle, blank circles indicate pupils who have not answered a question.

2. Volunteered and solicited answers: again in Box 7.2 circles represent pupils, use a 'V' for pupils who volunteer answers, and an 'A' for those who are asked to answer. Placing a sub-letter beside the 'V' or 'A' will indicate the sequence of the questioning (e.g. V1, A2, V3, V4, A5, A6, etc.).

BOX 7.2

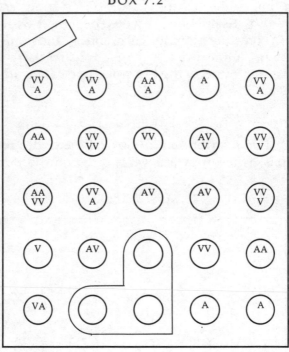

3. Verbatim recording of questioning transactions: record the questioning transactions using shorthand or shortened forms.

Teacher 'Turn 2 p 46. Mary give us y. ans. to q. 1.'

Mary 'WW II was partly t. result of unresolved conflicts of WW1.'

Teacher 'That's 1 pt. of the ans. John give us y. ans.'

4. Teacher response to questions answered: indicate how the teacher responds to answers by using the following abbreviations. Tally scores as in Box 7.3.

   V = verbal response
   NV = non-verbal response
   + = indicated positive response
   0 = indicated no response
   − = indicated negative response.

BOX 7.3

QUESTION	RESPONSE				
	V	NV	+	0	−
1	✔		✔		
2	✔		✔		
3		✔	✔		
4	✔				✔
5		✔		✔	
6	✔		✔		
7	✔		✔		
8	✔			✔	
9		✔	✔		
10		✔		✔	
Totals	6	4	6	3	1

Observing on-task/off-task behaviours

1. Identify, by scanning the classroom, all the students who appear to be off-task every two minutes. Number each scan, using the same number for all pupils who appear to be off-task during that scan. For example, during scan 7, five pupils appeared to be off-task as in Box 7.4.
2. Tally on-task/off-task behaviour: list in the off-task column, the number of pupils off-task at each scan (say every two minutes). Subtract the off-task from the class total to determine on-task pupils. Work out the percentages as in Box 7.5.
3. Tally observable off-task behaviour by using the following code:

BOX 7.4

BOX 7.5

SCAN	OFF-TASK		ON-TASK	
	Number	%	Number	%
1	4	16	21	84
2	6	24	19	76
3	1	4	24	96
4	0	0	25	100
5	3	12	22	88
6	3	12	22	88
7	6	24	19	76
8	5	20	20	80
9	4	16	21	84
10	4	16	21	84
Total	36		214	
Average		15		85

1. talking not related to task assigned
2. doodling
3. daydreaming
4. wandering around
5. working at other tasks
6. physically bothering other pupils
7. attempting to draw attention
8. pencil-sharpener, fountain, washroom
9. other.

This observation is easiest to do if you concentrate on a small number of pupils over an extended period, rather than trying to observe a whole class at once. During each scan (say every two minutes), observe the off-task behaviour and place the appropriate number in the space. If the student is on-task during the scan the space is left blank as seen in Box 7.6.

BOX 7.6

Student	SCAN										
	1	2	3	4	5	6	7	8	9	10	%
Polly	3	4				3		8			40
Kirsten	2	2		3	3		4	2	3	2	80
Marloes	6	7			6	6		7			40
David		5	5			5	5		5		50
Nancy	1	1	1	8				8	1		70

Interaction Checklists and Coding Scales

Although it may be preferable for teacher–researchers to devise their own observation scales, sometimes they may not have the time, or they may already be familiar with a coding scale previously invented that fits their purpose. In this section I will discuss a variety of coding scales that can be utilized in specific situations by teachers, and give a more detailed illustration of one interaction scale – the Flanders Interaction Analysis Categories.

The impetus for coding scales and checklists has come from North America where there is and has been a concern for 'scientific' approaches to teaching (Gage, 1978).

This 'scientific' approach is manifest in an emphasis on competency based teaching, behavioural objectives in curriculum planning and systematic instruction. It is unsurprising therefore to find that most coding scales available are American in origin. As Galton (1978) comments:

> The obvious starting point for any classification of inter-action analysis system must be *Mirrors for Behaviour* (Simon and Boyer, 1975). The current edition of this anthology contains some 200 observation schedules. Most are American and only two are British. In their collection the observation instruments are classified under eight main headings:
>
>   1. the subject of observation (teacher, pupil)
>   2. the setting under which the instrument is used (subject area)
>   3. the number of targets observed
>   4. the coding unit used
>   5. the collecting method employed
>   6. the number of observers required
>   7. the dimensions of the system (affective, cognitive)
>   8. the uses reported by the author.

One of the problems with many of American scales are that they are overly concerned with the formal teaching situation.

More recently, British researchers have been developing their own coding scales which, in general, stand in contrast to the American models. Galton (1978) comments again:

> A feature of British research has been the wide variety of different organisational contexts within which classroom observation has been carried out. Much criticism has been directed at American systems because they often seem appropriate only to the more formal type of teaching situation. One of the most interesting features of the British research is the emphasis on observation in informal settings at one extreme and the variety of schedules suitable for use in the microteaching setting for the purpose of evaluating performance in questioning and lecturing skills at the other.

These quotations from Galton (1978) are taken from his book *British Mirrors*, which is a collection of 41 classroom observation systems that are British in origin. The majority of these instruments are junior and secondary school oriented but some are specifically designed for infant or higher education settings. Their target is almost exclusively teachers and pupils, most require only one observer and they are almost exclusively concerned with descriptions of classroom practice. The four major foci of the instruments are: classroom climate, organizational learning, the management and control of routine activities, and knowledge content. In general they are applicable across all curriculum areas.

One of the earliest coding systems is the Flanders Interaction Analysis Categories (FIAC). Although it may not necessarily be the most effective of the systems available, it is probably the best known. It is widely used and has influenced the design of many other category systems.

FIAC is based on ten analytic categories that reflects Flander's conceptualization of teacher–pupil verbal interaction (see Figure 7.2). Each of the categories has a number, but no scale is implied.

In his book *Analyzing Teaching Behaviour*, Flanders (1970) described the ten categories in detail, but for our purposes the descriptions given in the illustration are sufficient. In order to help memorize the categories and make coding easier, one can shorten the descriptions of the categories as seen in Box 7.7.

The procedures for using the Flanders system are quite straightforward (more detail on the use of FIAC is found in the Open University (1976) course E 201 on which this discussion is based). Observers are first trained until they show a high level of agreement with other trained observers. Once they have been trained, they watch a lesson and apply the technique as follows using a coding sheet such as that illustrated in Figure 7.3.

1. Every three seconds the observer writes down the category best describing the verbal behaviour of the teacher and class.

Indirect influence	1.	Accepts feeling: accepts and clarifies the feeling tone of the student in a non-threatening manner. Feelings may be positive or negative. Predicting and recalling feelings are included.
	2.	Praises or encourages: praises or encourages student action or behaviour. Jokes that release tension, not at the expense of another individual, nodding head or saying 'uh huh?' or 'go on' are included
	3.	Accepts or uses ideas of student: clarifying, building, or developing ideas or suggestions by a student. As teacher brings more of his own ideas into play, shift to category five.
	4.	Asks questions: asking a question about content or procedure with the intent that a student answer.
Teacher talk	5.	Lectures: giving facts or opinions about content or procedures, expressing his own idea; asking rherorical questions.

Direct influence	6.	Gives directions: directions, commands, or orders with which a student is expected to comply.
	7.	Criticizes or justifies authority: statements, intended to change student behaviour from non-acceptable to acceptable pattern; bawling someone out; stating why the teacher is doing what he is doing, extreme self-reference.
Student talk	8.	Student talk-response: talk by students in response to teacher. Teacher initiates the contact or solicits student statement.
	9.	Student talk-initiation: talk by students, which they initiate. If 'calling on' student is only to indicate who may talk next, observer must decide whether student wanted to talk. If he did, use this category.
	10.	Silence or confusion: pauses, short periods of silence, and periods of confusion in which communication cannot be understood by the observer.

FIGURE 7.2 *Flanders interaction analysis categories*

BOX 7.7

Teacher talk	1.	accepts feelings
	2.	praise
	3.	accepts ideas
	4.	question
	5.	lecture
	6.	command
	7.	criticism
Pupil talk	8.	solicited
	9.	unsolicited
	10.	silence

2. The numbers are written in sequence across the data sheet.
3. Each line of the data sheet contains twenty squares, thus representing approximately one minute of time.
4. Separate 'episodes' can be identified by scribbled margin notes, and a new line commenced for a new 'episode'.
5. In a research project the observer would have a pocket timer designed to give a signal every three seconds, thus reminding him or her to record a tally (a stop-watch or the second hand of a wristwatch can be used).

Two main advantages of the Flanders system are that it is fairly easy to learn and apply, and that the ten categories describe a number of behaviours which many would agree are important, such as the teacher's use of praise and criticism and the pupil's solicited and unsolicited talk. In addition, the tallying of events every three seconds enables considerable information to be collected and analysed. There is usually a high agreement between trained observers.

On the other hand much information is lost, especially non-verbal aspects of communication. In particular, some categories are too broad, (e.g. category 4), and others discriminate insufficiently. For example, category 5 does not discriminate between giving information which is correct and that which is incorrect. Category 10 can repre-

School _____   Teacher_____
Class _____   Subject _____
Date _____   Observer _____
Lesson (1st, 2nd, etc.)___

TALLY ACROSS

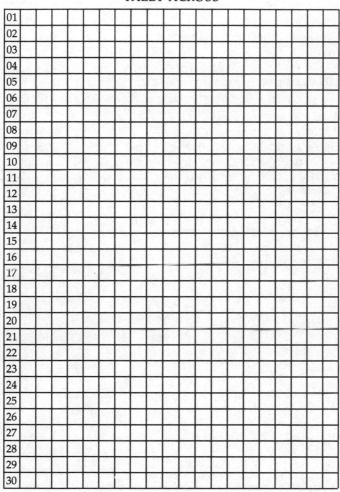

FIGURE 7.3 *FIAC Lesson Observation Sheet*

sent both the silence achieved by an autocrat and the chaos which occurs when a teacher has lost control. Also, there are too few pupil categories, and it is difficult to use in informal classrooms, where two or more members may be talking at once.

For our purposes, FIAC is most appropriately used as a means for gathering classroom data that can then be used as a basis for action. So, for example, if after using FIAC a teacher discovered that s/he was talking too much then that becomes an identifiable problem upon which action can be taken and monitored by classroom research procedures.

A simple example illustrates the first few seconds of an exchange occuring in the twelfth minute of a lesson.

The teacher tells children to look at a map on page 60 of their books and asks the name of the country coloured green. There is a short pause and then a child replied. The text of this exchange and the data sheet would look like that shown in Box 7.8.

BOX 7.8

		Category number tallied by observer
Teacher:	'Look at the map on page 60.'	6 (command)
Teacher:	'What is the country coloured green?'	4 (question)
	three-second pause	10 (silence)
Pupil:	'I think it's Finland, but I'm not sure.'	8 (solicited pupil talk)

Data sheet entry (minute 12 of the lesson)	12	6	4	10	8

Commentary

This chapter has been concerned with a variety of approaches to classroom observation. I have described them in sequence ranging from the most *ad hoc* (peer observation) to the most structured and specific (interaction schedules). These approaches contrast with those described in the previous chapter in two important ways. First, they require the presence of an observer in the classroom. Second, they are more focused in so far as they are concerned with specific aspects of a teacher's behaviour rather than a general diagnostic exploration of one's own teaching.

There are some potential problems in the use of these approaches, particularly the interaction scales. The first is that each scale represents the author's concept of a situation. One is looking at classrooms through someone else's eyes, and their purposes and perceptions could be very different from one's own. It is easy, therefore, to get trapped within the intentions of the researcher who designed the scale. Consequently, it is important for the teacher–researcher to match his/her needs closely to the intent and focus of the scale. In that way the teacher–researcher can maintain control over the situation. The second problem is that most scales were not designed for use by teachers. Their original intent was mainly as research tools for analysing classrooms. Within the context of this book, however, it is important to stress that they are tools teachers can use to improve practice. The teacher–researchers' orientation is always action.

Further Reading

The two collections of classroom observation schedules by Simon and Boyer (1975) and Galton (1978) are primary sources for teacher–researchers wanting detail of coding scales. Good & Brophy's *Looking in Classrooms* (1978), contains many schedules for measuring classroom behaviour: this book is an important resource for teacher–researchers as it presents much recent material on teaching skills and provides ways of assessing it in practical situations. Chanan and Delamont (1975) give a useful account of British work in the area. The Open University (1976) course E201 *Personality and Learning* (Block II) contains a very thorough review of the Flanders System. The most useful resource on clinical supervision for our purposes is Acheson and Gall's *Techniques in the Clinical Supervision of Teachers* (1980). The classic texts on clinical supervision are by Goldhammer *et al.* (1980) and Cogan (1973). Walker and Adelman (1975) also contains useful information on classroom observation.

8

Analysing Classroom Research Data

The third criterion for teacher research outlined in chapter four was that the methodology employed must be reliable enough to allow teachers to confidently formulate hypotheses and develop strategies applicable to their classroom situations. This is an area where teacher research has not been conspicuously successful. Consequently, it is important to establish a coherent methodology for analysing classroom research data. In this chapter, I first outline the problem in a little more detail, then suggest a framework for analysis and describe the four stages that comprise the process.

The Problem

Action research, like most practitioner oriented methodologies, has been widely criticized, but mainly by those who implicitly denigrate the method by criticizing individual research projects that have adopted classroom research techniques. It is illogical, not to say unfair, to judge the quality of a Shakespeare play by observing a performance by amateur actors. And so it is with classroom research. It is true though that classroom research is often done badly. Confusion between the independent and dependent variables is the most common reason for invalidating action research efforts. Also, the methodology of teacher-based classroom research is, in general, not clearly articulated and consequently, it is carried out sloppily. What follows is an attempt to rectify this situation.

The issue of handling data in action research situations is a contentious one. The rules for quasi-experimental research have been cogently articulated (Campbell and Stanley, 1963) and have a long and distinguished tradition. This tradition is so prevalent that research in education is commonly equated with studies carried out under this paradigm. This should not be surprising for the rules are simple to apply and are consistent with the ubiquitous psycho-statistical research tradition. It is unfortunate, as we have seen, that this approach is ill-suited to the research needs of the classroom teacher. In classroom research, the concern is more with cases than samples. This implies a methodology more applicable to understanding a problematic situation than one based on predicting outcomes within the parameters of an existing and tacitly accepted social system.

A Framework for Analysis

Making sense of social situations has long been the task of sociologists and it is from their (and anthropologists') methodological canons that much recent avant-garde work on educational evaluation has been drawn (*vide*, Hamilton *et al*, 1977). It is this research tradition that provides a framework within which to consider teacher-based classroom research. Classrooms are also complex social situations that require understanding. We need to produce theory that is applicable to classrooms as well as within them.

Two of the classic statements on sociological fieldwork were made by Becker (1958) and Glaser and Strauss (1967). In his paper 'Problems of inference and proof in participant observation', Becker (1958, 653) describes four stages in the analysis of fieldwork data:

We can distinguish three distinct stages of analysis conducted in the field itself, and a fourth stage, carried on after completion of the field work. These stages are differentiated, first, by their logical sequence: each succeeding stage depends on some analysis in the preceding stage. They are further differentiated by the fact that different kinds of conclusions are arrived at in each stage and that these conclusions are put to different uses in the continuing research. Finally, they are differentiated by the different criteria that are used to assess evidence and to reach conclusions in each stage. The three stages of field analysis are: the selection and definition of problems, concepts, and indices; the check on the frequency and distribution of phenomena; and the incorporation of individual findings into a model of the organisation under study. The fourth stage of final analysis involves problems of presentation of evidence and proof.

In a similar way, Glaser and Strauss (1967, 105) describe in *The Discovery of Grounded Theory* the concept of the constant comparative method as a means of analysing sociological data:

We shall describe in four stages the constant comparative method; 1. comparing incidents applicable to each category, 2. integrating categories and their properties, 3. delimiting the theory, and 4. writing the theory. Although this method of generating theory is a continuously growing process – each stage after a time is transformed into the next – earlier stages do remain in operation simultaneously throughout the analysis and each provides continuous development to its successive stage until the analysis is terminated.

Although Glaser and Strauss' notion of the constant comparative method is a more dynamic concept than Becker's linear sequence of stages, there are basic similarities in their approaches to the analysis of field data. Each envisage the analytic process as having four distinct generic stages: 1. data collection and the initial generation of categories, 2. validation of categories, 3. interpretation of categories, and 4. action. These various stages are summarized in Figure 8.1 and represent standard practice for the analysis of qualitative field data. My major

Classroom Research	Becker	Glaser & Strauss
• Data collection	• Selection and definition of concepts	• Compare incidents applicable to each category
• Validation	• Frequency and distribution of concepts	• Integrate categories and their phenomena
• Interpretation	• Incorporation of findings into model	• Delimit theory
• Action	• Presentation of evidence and proof	• Write theory

FIGURE 8.1　*Fieldwork methodology*

point is that this same process can be used by teachers to analyse data emerging from their own classroom research efforts.

Jane: an example

As part of the requirements for a course I taught on the 'Analysis of Teaching', Jane made a videotape of herself experimenting with various models of teaching. After reviewing the videotape, Jane felt that among other observations she had been rather abrupt in her questioning technique and had given the pupils little time to formulate responses to her questions. I suggested to Jane that she explore this observation a little further and ascertain whether this was a consistent behaviour or an aberration. She did this by taking a further videotape of her teaching, and by asking a colleague to observe her teaching. Jane also developed a short questionnaire on her questioning technique, which she administered to her pupils and subsequently analysed. As a result of this endeavour, Jane realized that she did in fact interject very quickly after asking a question, and quite often answered her own questions. All well and good, Jane thought, but what does this mean? Thinking that recent research on teaching might help, Jane did some reading and came across an article on think-time. The article reviewed a number of studies on the relationship between the amount of time that elapsed after questioning and the quality of pupil response. Jane felt that she was not allowing her pupils enough time to think after she had asked a question to the detriment perhaps of their level of cognitive functioning. So she developed a plan to change and monitor her questioning technique. It took Jane some six months to complete these tasks (teaching is a time consuming job!), but there was no pressure on her to complete the research. In fact, the longer time frame allowed for more valid data, and she was pleased with the results. Not only did she find evidence of higher level responses from her pupils, but also, by involving them in the evoluation of her teaching, the climate of her class was enhanced by the mutual and overt commitment of both teacher and pupils to the learning process.

Data Collection

In the classroom research process, the first step is collecting data. With the use of say a video tape recorder the teacher gathers information about his or her teaching behaviour. Having collected the data, a substage follows immediately or co-exists with the collection of data – the generation of hypotheses. We are always generating hypotheses to explain classroom events. Even at the earliest stages of research, we are interpreting and explaining to ourselves 'why this is happening' and 'what caused that'. It is inevitable that as individuals we bring our experience and beliefs to bear upon situations that we wish to understand better. As Popper says, 'observations ... are always interpretations of the facts observed ... they are interpretations in the light of theories' (quoted in Magee, 1973, 107). Popper's use of the word theory implies, of course, not only 'grand' theory, but also personal theory – the presuppositions, assumptions and beliefs that guide our actions.

At the end of the data collection stage, not only have we collected our data, but we have also established a number of hypotheses that begin to explain what is happening in the classroom. These hypotheses usually emerge quite naturally from the data gathering process. Jane, in the example, generated a number of ideas about her teaching from viewing the video tape. Amongst these was an observation that she was too abrupt in her questioning technique and had given her pupils too little time to answer questions. These hypotheses not only reflect the data but are also an interpretation of it. At this stage, the more hypotheses the better. The richer and more creative our thoughts the more likely it is that the research will result in a coherent and complete interpretation of the problem. It is in the following stage that we begin to evaluate the hypotheses, so initially feel free to be as creative and as suggestive as you can.

Validation

The second stage in the process concerns the validation of the hypotheses. I will suggest two techniques for

establishing the validity of an hypotheses. One is saturation, the other is triangulation.

Let me begin with saturation. Becker, and Glaser and
Strauss point to a similar process: Becker refers to 'the
check on the frequency and distribution of phenomenon'
(1958, 653) and Glaser and Strauss to 'saturation' a situation where 'no additional data are being found ... (to)
develop properties of the category' (1967, 67). When
applied to the classroom research situation, this implies
that the hypothesis or category generated from observation is tested repeatedly against the data in an attempt to
modify or falsify it.

It is difficult and perhaps reckless to suggest a frequency
that ensures the validity of a category for that will vary
from case to case, but during this process a number of
predictable events can occur. First, if on repeated testing
the category is found wanting it is then discarded.
Second, the category may have been conceptualized
crudely and through testing, the concept is modified,
refined and amplified. Third, although the process of
falsification (in the Popperian sense) is never complete,
there comes a time when repeated observation leads
neither to refutation nor amplification and only serves to
support the hypothesis. At this point, when the utility of
observation decreases, saturation can be said to have
occurred and the hypothesis has been validated.

Referring to the example of Jane, having decided to
explore her questioning technique further, she videotaped
herself again and found that, in fact, she was quite abrupt
in her questioning and interjected far too quickly. In this
way, she firmly validated the observation by saturating it.

The other important technique for validation is triangulation. This concept was popularized by John Elliott and
Clem Adelman during their work with the Ford Teaching
Project. It involves contrasting the perceptions of one
actor in a specific situation against those of other actors in
the same situation. By doing this, an initial subjective
observation or perception is fleshed out and given a
degree of authenticity. Elliott and Adelman (1976, 74)
describe the technique thus:

> Triangulation involves gathering accounts of a teaching
> situation from three quite different points of view; namely,

those of the teacher, his pupils, and a participant observer. Who in the 'triangle' gathers the accounts, how they are elicited, and who compares them, depends largely on the context. The process of gathering accounts from three distinct standpoints has an epistemological justification. Each point of the triangle stands in a unique epistemological position with respect to access to relevant data about a teaching situation. The teacher is in the best position to gain access via introspection to his own intentions and aims in the situation. The students are in the best position to explain how the teacher's actions influence the way they respond in the situation. The participant observer is in the best position to collect data about the observable features of the interaction between teachers and pupils. By comparing his own account with accounts from the other two standpoints a person at one point of the triangle has an opportunity to test and perhaps revise it on the basis of more sufficient data.

Besides saturating the observation, Jane also validated it through triangulation. She had another teacher observe her teaching and she also gave her pupils a questionnaire on her questioning technique. From this evidence, she was able to validate and refine the observation from three different sources.

It must be admitted that triangulation is not always an easy process to engage in. Initially, it may be threatening for a teacher to involve students in the evaluation of their teaching, or it may prove difficult to obtain the services of a peer to act as a participant observer. Teachers with the personal openness and interest in their teaching needed to initiate such research will, however, eventually overcome these difficulties. Incidentally, I believe that it is important for the teacher to involve his or her pupils in the research process as soon as their confidence allows. Children provide wonderfully frank and honest feedback, especially when they sense that their opinions are valued and respected, and this can only serve to enhance the quality of life in the classroom. The teacher must, however, be careful to introduce this change in his or her teaching slowly and self-consciously, being fully aware that pupils are a potentially conservative force within the classroom and often need to be 'broken in' to new ideas and different styles (Rudduck, 1984).

Let me now restate the important methodological point. I am arguing that by employing analytic techniques such as saturation and triangulation on classroom data, teacher–researchers can produce hypotheses and concepts that are valid, methodologically sound and to an extent generalizable. By engaging in this process of hypothesis generation, teacher–researchers are producing what Glaser and Strauss have called grounded theory, because it is theory grounded in data gathered from and applicable to a specific social situation. By utilizing this methodology, we can have confidence in our subsequent actions for, as Dunn and Swierczek (1977, 137) comment:

> The application of grounded theories promises to contribute to improvements in the degree to which findings 1. reflect conditions actually present in particular change efforts (internal validity); 2. typify conditions actually present in other change efforts (external validity); 3. contribute to the generation of new concepts by constantly comparing information obtained by different methods (reflexivity); and 4. promote understanding among groups with conflicting frames of reference.

Interpretation

The third stage in the research process is interpretation. This involves taking a validated hypothesis and fitting it into a frame of reference that gives it meaning. For the classroom researcher, this means taking a hypothesis and relating it either to theory, the norms of accepted practice or the teacher's own intuition as to what comprises good teaching. This allows the teacher–researcher to give meaning to a particular observation or series of observations that can lead profitably to action. In doing this, the classroom researcher is creating meaning out of hitherto discrete observations and constructs.

Jane gave meaning to her hypothesis by reading about 'think time'. That information not only helped her understand the implications of her behaviour but also suggested a direction for action.

Action

The final step in the process is action. Having created meaning out of the research data, the teacher–researcher is in a position to plan for future action. Building on the evidence gathered during the research, the teacher is able to plan realistic strategies which are themselves monitored by classroom research procedures. Jane did just that. The interpretation stage gave her information on how to change her questioning technique which after some planning she attempted to monitor and evaluate.

Commentary

The analysis of data is a very important part of the classroom research process. It is only at this stage that the teacher can be certain that the results obtained are valid and reliable. Often teacher–researchers fail to analyse adequately their data and thus lack a secure platform for action. The four stages of classroom research are outlined in Box 8.1.

Box 8.1

Four Stages of Classroom Research
1. **Data Collection** and the generation of hypotheses
2. **Validation** of hypotheses using the techniques of saturation and triangulation.
3. **Interpretation** by reference to theory, established practice or teacher judgement.
4. **Action** for improvement that is also monitored by classroom research techniques.

The four stages of classroom research, although based on sociological research methods, are, in fact, only organized common sense. Can you think of a classroom situation where you have intuitively applied these stages?

Further Reading

Since the mid-seventies, there has been a growing interest in illuminative, anthropological and ethnographic research approaches. Much of this literature is technical and not ideally suited for our purposes. However, a recent book by Hammersley and Atkinson (1983), *Ethnography: Principles in Practice*, provides an excellent overview of the field and an introduction to the literature. Guba's (1978) monograph, *Towards a Methodology of Naturalistic Inquiry in Educational Evaluation*, is also a useful source. *Beyond the Numbers Game* (Hamilton *et al.* 1977) is a comprehensive statement on the illuminative or new wave tradition in educational evaluation and research; the discussion of alternative methodology, especially the work of Louis Smith, is particularly valuable. Clem Adelman's book. *Uttering, Muttering* (1981), on linguistic research in classrooms contains an excellent chapter on triangulation. In addition, the references mentioned in the text should be consulted, especially Becker (1958) and Glaser and Strauss (1967), although the latter may prove to be a little hard going. Anyone seriously interested in educational research should also be familiar with Campbell and Stanley's (1963) classic 'Experimental and quasi-experimental designs for research on teaching'. Although written with a different perspective from this book, its discussion of research designs and the concepts of reliability and validity are exemplary and essential knowledge for those involved in educational research.

9

Maintaining the Action

The link between research and action has been an implicit theme throughout this book. To teacher–researchers, research is a necessary but not sufficient condition for professional development. In this context, research inevitably feeds action and improvement. The classroom research process described in previous chapters has as its goal professional development and the improvement of classroom performance. The fourth stage in the analytic framework discussed in the last chapter was action, this being the crowning achievement of the research process. And that action is itself monitored and researched using classroom research procedures.

In this chapter, I want to look at some of the ways in which the action, generated by the research process, can be maintained. I will be discussing how teacher–researchers go about reporting their research, some issues involved in publication, the nature of collaborative action, curriculum and pedagogy, and ways in which teacher research fits with current demands for school evaluation and teacher accreditation.

Reporting the Research

There are a number of different ways of reporting teacher research efforts (*vide*, Nixon, 1981). I have seen them range from loose anecdotal accounts to highly 'scientific' and formal research reports submitted for a higher degree. In many instances, teachers who engage in classroom research have no need to present their results to anyone except to themselves, particularly if the research is to be used solely for improving their teaching. Despite this, I think that all teacher–researchers need to put their data together in such a way that:

1. the research could be replicated on another occasion
2. the evidence used to generate hypotheses and consequent action is clearly documented
3. action taken as a result of the research is monitored.

This process of setting a clear purpose, of using a methdology which provides valid results, and then using these as a basis for action can be made relatively straightforward if the researcher keeps a loose leaf log or diary as the research progresses. In my classroom research course, I ask the teachers to prepare a report on their research using as a guide the points contained in Figure 9.1. The purpose of this is to provide them with a

---

1. *Statement of Intent*
   - clarify purpose
   - rationale

2 *Procedures and Process*
   - research design
   - techniques of data collection
   - verification of concepts
   - what actually occurred

3. *Results and Implementation*
   - outcomes of research
   - theoretical implications
   - action taken as a result
   - evaluation of action

4. *Meta Analysis*
   - review whole process
   - conclusions as to utility of research
   - what would you do different next time

FIGURE 9.1 *Writing the research report*

---

framework for their research. Whilst this is important, what perhaps is even more critical is that it encourages the teacher to stand back and to examine systematically the process by making a meta-analysis of the research.

Publication and Research

Mention of writing a research report raises the question of publication. As a precursor to the discussion let me quote from Ebbutt (1983):

> If action research is to be considered legitimately as research, the participants in it must, it seems to me, be prepared to produce written reports of their activities. Moreover these reports ought to be available to some form of public critique. I would go as far as to say that if this condition is not satisfied by participants then no matter how personally and professionally valuable the exercise is in which they are engaged, it is not action research.

Whilst I would agree with Ebbutt's call for written reports and critique, particularly by other teacher–researchers, I disagree with the implication that unless the research is published it is not research. It seems to me that many current commentators on classroom research have a misplaced conception of what research actually is.

An example of this is Jon Nixon's A Teacher's Guide to Action Research (1981). It is a collection of teacher research reports loosely gathered together, and varying in quality. Many of the essays are anecdotal and subjective, and provide no critical commentary on the process or behaviours they purport to describe. 'That's alright', its apologists claim, 'because it is not research, it is enquiry or self monitoring'. And this is exactly the problem.

Michael Armstrong (1982) makes the distinction in a most beguiling way:

> I have grown impatient with the concept of 'research'. In the context of a study of education it has acquired too narrow a connotation especially in regard to criteria for rigour, evidence and validity. I prefer the word 'enquiry' ... The form of enquiry which I have in mind is grounded

in the experience of teaching and in particular in that
practice of sustained observation which is inseparable from
good teaching ...

Armstrong seems to be saying, 'Let's call it enquiry and
let's keep it in the classroom and then we won't need to
tangle with such questions as what counts as research'.
Hull *et al* (1985), complicate this position even further.
They appear to say, 'let's call what Armstrong does self-
monitoring (an investigation of one's own practice in
private) but let's recognise that there is also teacher
research'. They argue that teacher research:

> ... must feed a tradition – from which individual re-
> searchers can derive support. In this way it is quite
> different from the activity which has been called 'self-
> monitoring' where a teacher uses some of the data-
> gathering techniques developed by researchers to record
> instances of their own practice as a basis for reflection. The
> self-monitoring teacher makes no claims to be
> methodologically reflexive. He or she does not undertake
> responsibility either to introduce 'system' into the investi-
> gations or make accounts of the studies available to other
> teachers. Self-monitoring is essentially a privatised en-
> counter between a practitioner and practice. As such it has
> immense value. We conceive teacher research however, as
> potentially the root of a tradition of enquiry into educa-
> tional processes which might stand alongside the academic
> tradition as an alternative body of knowledge rooted firmly
> in practice.

This statement is confused and problematic. The
dichotomy that Armstrong and Hull point to is just not
there.

Armstrong's *Closely Observed Children* (1980) is probably
the best of the second generation of teacher research
studies. It is sensitive, insightful and profound; it is
research at a high level of sophistication, imagination
and rigour. Armstrong is doing teacher research and
himself in particular a grave disservice to claim otherwise.
One can readily appreciate Armstrong's 'impatience with
the concept of research' – but to call it something else is
not to change anything. He is impatient of narrowly

defined psycho-statistical research that has little to say to teachers, not research per se.

Research, enquiry, and self-monitoring are all aspects of a similar activity because they all require systematic, self-conscious and rigorous reflection to be of any value. The problem is that psychological research with its emphasis on statistical manipulation has captured the educational imagination to such an extent that most people cannot think of research in any other terms. But criteria, such as validity, reliability and generalizability, are necessary if teacher–researchers are to escape the sentimental anecdote that often replaces statistical research designs in education, and gives teacher research such a bad name. Enquiry, self-monitoring, and teacher research need to establish standards and criteria that are applicable to their area of activity, rather than assume (and then reject) criteria designed for different procedures.

Teacher research like enquiry and self monitoring, is a form of research. These forms may be presented to different audiences and formulated in different ways, but all are attempts to create meaning out of complex situations. And the meaning is only valid when it is subject to certain methodological standards. It is naive to argue that just because we call what we do enquiry or self monitoring instead of research that we can escape the demand for valid judgement. That is throwing the baby out with the bath water. But, it is equally incorrect to assume that just because we engage in research, we have to follow the criteria of the psycho-statistical research paradigm. These criteria are inappropriate, and other more suitable methods, like the ones discussed in the previous chapter, have to be sought.

There are two important points to be drawn from this discussion. The first is that classroom research by teachers is a valid form of research because it results in hypotheses generated through a rigorous process of enquiry and grounded in the data to which they apply. This meets contemporary criteria for research. In the article to which I have already referred, Ebbutt (1983) quotes:

> Shulman's conception of what counts as research; that it is 'a family of methods which share the characteristics of disciplined inquiry' ...

1. arguments and evidence can be examined
2. not dependent solely on eloquence or surface plausibility
3. avoids sources of error when possible and discusses margin for possible errors in conclusion
4. can be speculative, free wheeling and inventive.

This, it seems to me, is an accurate description of research as it has been described in this book.

The second point is that it is important for teacher–researchers to open up their work to critique and, if possible, to publish it. The importance of public critique in classroom research is that it encourages a discourse among teachers which is research oriented, and committed to action and the improvement of practice. It is the sharing of our experiences and the social and intellectual benefits that emanate from it, not the meeting of some abstract academic criteria, that provide the logic for publication and critique in classroom research. But the important point is that the mere fact of publication cannot be a judgement on the nature of the process that led (or did not lead) to publication.

Collaborative Action

Sharing and collaboration among teacher–researchers is critical. Each of the case studies reported in chapter two involved or mentioned collaboration in classroom research and so highlighted its importance. Scattered throughout the examples in the book are illustrations of the ways in which teachers can support each other in classroom research efforts and the benefits all of those involved gain from it.

It is passé to talk about the 'sanctity of the classroom door' and the isolation that teachers work in. But, despite the various innovations in team teaching in the sixties and seventies, the classroom remains very much an individual preserve. Yet it is well established that teachers learn best from other teachers, so this vast potential for mutual improvement remains largely untapped. Another aspect of collaboration is that teacher research, at least initially, is fairly threatening and often goes against the work and professional norms of a school. The involvement of another teacher in the research process greatly alleviates the sense of isolation and contributes towards increased purpose and commitment.

There are four specific ways in which collaborative action for classroom research by teachers can be maintained: through school based professional development, attendance at inservice courses, the establishment of informal clubs and networks, and the inclusion of pupils in the research process.

It is unfortunate that we have not yet built an infrastructure for professional development within our schools (*vide*, McKibbin and Joyce, 1980). Such an infrastructure would involve portions of the school week being devoted to professional development activities such as curriculum development, training sessions for curriculum implementation and new models of teaching, regular observation/ clinical supervision sessions, and on-site coaching amongst other activities. Integral to these activities is a commitment to reviewing one's performance as a prelude to improvement. It is within this context that classroom research is a fundamental professional development activity. Although this scenario is not the norm in many schools, it is in some, and the image is well known and motivating (Joyce *et al.*, 1983). Teacher research has a part to play in moving towards this goal.

Short inservice courses are still the dominant mode of professional development in the United Kingdom. Although the limitations of 'one shot' workshops and courses for developing new skills and teaching strategies are well known (Joyce and Showers, 1980), they still have some value (Rudduck, 1981). Such courses provide an easy way to gain information about teacher research, they often provide a forum for the sharing of experience, and many courses provide some opportunities for practice and feedback. Perhaps most importantly, they offer opportunities for networking and possibilities for future collaboration with other teachers. In the institution where I work, for example, I offer a 'mini-course' on teacher research that deals with the knowledge and skills discussed in this book. The Cambridge Institute of Education, the base of the Ford Teaching project, regularly runs courses on teacher research, and the Classroom Action Research Network (see Appendix A) also sponsors courses and conferences on classroom research by teachers.

It is also not unknown for groups of teachers to form an *ad hoc* group (based perhaps on the local teachers centre) that acts as a 'club' for teacher–researchers. Groups such as this, although not prolific, are an important potential resource for those teachers wishing to engage in classroom research and professional development activities. Other forms of networking emerge in local areas and serve the teachers in them.

Another potential source of collaborative action are the pupils in one's own classroom. I have already mentioned the usefulness of pupil feedback for triangulation purposes, and the spin off in terms of positive climate that occurs when pupils are involved in classroom research. I want to stress that point again here. It is entirely within the spirit of classroom research that pupils be involved in the process of improving the teaching–learning situation in their classrooms. The rewards for doing that for the teacher and the general ethos of the class are significant. Recently, I read a large number of classroom research projects by teachers and was struck by the number of times they mentioned the importance of this aspect of their research. It must be added, however, that pupils need to be introduced to the concept carefully and incrementally. Sudden and radical changes in classroom norms, even if they are for wholly admirable and democratic purposes, can be threatening to pupils unless they have been prepared for it (Rudduck, 1984).

Curriculum and Pedagogy

In the previous section, I alluded to other forms of professional development that have a bearing on teacher research. Curriculum development and models of teaching are very much part of that, and the approach to classroom research being advocated here has a particular relevance to curriculum and teaching.

Most centralized school systems prescribe what is to be taught to pupils but require the teacher to implement the curriculum. Unfortunately, most teachers have had little exposure to different teaching strategies and this limits their flexibility in and control of their professional situation. This reinforces to themselves and others the image of the teacher as technician. More emphasis on differing teaching styles and on research oriented teaching would result in teachers who are more confident, flexible, and autonomous.

In chapter five, I made reference to a Stenhouse suggestion that classroom research be used as a means of testing curriculum ideas. The context of that proposal is worth reproducing in full (Stenhouse 1975, 142–143):

> I have argued that educational ideas expressed in books are not easily taken into possession by teachers, whereas the expression of ideas as curricular specifications exposes them to testing by teachers and hence establishes an equality of discourse between the proposer and those who assess his proposal. There is, of course, no implication as to the origins of the proposal or hypotheses being tested. The originator may be a classroom teacher, a policy-maker or an educational research worker. The crucial point is that the proposal is not to be regarded as an unqualified recommendation but rather as a provisional specification claiming no more than to be worth putting to the test of practice. Such proposals claim to be intelligent rather than correct.
>
> I have identified a curriculum as a particular form of specification about the practice of teaching and not as a package of materials of a syllabus of ground to be covered. It is a way of translating any educational idea into a hypothesis testable in practice. It invites critical testing rather than acceptance.
>
> I have reached towards a research design based upon these ideas, implying that a curriculum is a means of studying the problems and effects of implementing any defined line of teaching.
>
> The uniqueness of each classroom setting implies that any proposal – even at school level – needs to be tested and verified and adapted by each teacher in his own classroom. The ideal is that the curricular specification should feed a teacher's personal research and development programme through which he is progessively increasing his understanding of his own work and hence bettering his teaching.
>
> To summarize the implications of this position, all well-founded curriculum research and development, whether

the work of an individual teacher, of a school, or of a group working in a teachers' centre or of a group working within the co-ordinating framework of a national project, is based on the study of classrooms. It thus rests on the work of teachers.

Here Stenhouse is linking classroom research by teachers firmly to the curriculum and teaching. This is an important point that may have been lost in all the talk about the gathering and analysis of data. Teacher research is not an end in itself but is inextricably linked to curriculum change and the adoption of new teaching strategies. It is a vehicle for curriculum reform and improvement. For example, teacher–researchers were involved in the Humanities Project in monitoring the utility of a curriculum and in the Ford Teaching Project in examining enquiry/discovery teaching approaches. In both instances, teacher research was linked to a substantive educational issue.

Teacher Research and the Control of Education

The past five to ten years have seen increasing controls being placed on the schooling system in the United Kingdom. A majority of local education authorities have initiated schemes for the evaluation of schools for accountability purposes. And at the present time similar plans are being drawn up for the accreditation of teachers. There is, of course, nothing wrong *per se* about school evaluation, but the unfortunate aspect of most accountability schemes is their control orientation which often has a negative impact on teacher professionalism. Amongst the values implicit in teacher research is an opposition to centralized control of education and a commitment to teacher and school autonomy. One way of resolving this dichotomy is to emphasize more professional forms of accountability; to encourage schools and teachers to become accountable to professional codes of practice or principles rather than to examination results or arbitrary product criteria (which in any case are notoriously difficult to establish). Sockett (1980, 19) distinguishes between accountability for results, and accountability in terms of professional codes of practice:

> If we notice the difference between a system based on results and a system based on principles, the characterizing differences of an alternative can be seen as follows:
>
> 1. accountability would be for adherence to principles of practice rather than for results embodied in pupil performances,
> 2. accountability would be rendered to diverse constituencies rather than to the agglomerate constituency of the public alone,
> 3. the teacher would have to be regarded as an autonomous professional, not as a social technician, within the bureaucratic framework of a school and the educational system,
> 4. the evaluation through measurement of pupil performances (the 'how' of accountability) would be replaced by a conception of evaluation as providing information for constituents allied to a system of proper redress through a professional body.

The implications of this for teacher–researchers are clear. Teacher research is professionalism par excellence; the challenge is to capitalize on current demands for accountability by emphasizing professionalism rather than some arbitrary output criteria. In that way, not only will teacher research be boosted, but we will also have moved a long way along the road towards establishing a professional ethic for teaching.

Commentary

The initial theme of this chapter was the issue of publishing classroom research, where publication is understood as the public sharing and critique of teacher research, particularly by other teacher–researchers. I then argued strenuously against those who claim that teacher research is not really research. Their position is untenable because 1. it is a capitulation in the face of the norms of traditional research, 2. it devalues the quality of teacher research efforts, and 3. it avoids the necessity of establishing a rigorous methodology for classroom research.

I then discussed ways in which the momentum engendered by classroom research by teachers can be sustained, and influence the wider educational scene. The initial steps are monitoring one's research efforts, discussing them with other teachers, and building informal support structures for teacher research. These steps are within the control of teachers, as is the linking of their research work with substantive educational issues related to curriculum and pedagogy.

More problematic, however, is the establishing of an infrastructure for professional development and the threat to teacher professionalism by contemporary demands for acountability. There are no easy solutions to these problems, but one approach is through establishing a professional ethic for teaching that has as a central component classroom research by teachers.

Further Reading

The notion of collaborative action and its implications for professional development has been the focus of much of Bruce Joyce's work (e.g. Joyce *et al.* 1981, 1983, Joyce and Showers, 1984). The potential for utilizing school evaluation for developmental purposes has been explored by Nuttall (1981) and Hopkins (1985). An example of how this can be achieved in practice is provided by the Schools Council GRIDS project (McMahon *et al.* 1984). In a reader for the Open University course on evaluation and accountability, McCormick (1982) includes a number of articles on this theme and others that have a direct relevance to classroom research by teachers.

10

A Final Word

A continuing theme throughout the book has been the establishing of a professional ethic for teaching. Implicit in this idea is the concept of teacher as researcher. This image may be unfamiliar to those imbued with the notion of teacher as technician – someone who has mastered certain skills for classroom control and learnt techniques for teaching particular subjects but in the main is accountable to others for putting into practice ideas developed elsewhere. Unfortunately one can characterize teaching, in most of Europe and in North America in this way, as being a form of alienated labour, with teachers comprising a sub group lacking in professional autonomy, denied control over their form of work and relegated to a purely instrumental role. It is unsurprising therefore if the image of the teacher–researcher is unfamiliar, for as a concept it embodies features that value responsibility, critical reflection and the exercise of professional judgement. It is only the teacher who can create good teaching, and if we envisage teaching as a process that values the maximization of individual potential, then the values implicit in the teacher–research image are paramount.

The teacher–researcher image is a powerful one. It embodies a number of characteristics that reflect on the individual teacher's capacity to be in Stenhouse's phrase 'autonomous in professional judgement'. A major factor in this is the teacher's ability to theorize about practice, and to think systematically and critically about what he or she is doing. Central to this activity is the systematic reflection on one's classroom experience, to understand it and to create meaning out of that understanding. This involves taking steps to ensure that one's judgements are not coloured by prejudice, whimsy or arbitrariness, and that the generation of hypotheses about one's own teaching are based on reliable procedures that are also open to public scrutiny.

Ultimately, this is what this book is about; it is an attempt to enable teachers to become more self-conscious, systematic and critical about their teaching with the aim of improving it. By so doing teachers will develop more power over their professional lives and be better able to create classrooms and schools more responsive to the vision they and we have for our children's future.

References

Acheson, K. and Gall, M. (1980). *Techniques in the Clinical Supervision of Teachers*. New York, Longman.

Adelman, C. (1981). *Uttering, Muttering*. London, Grant McIntyre.

Armstrong, M. (1980). *Closely Observed Children*. London, Writers and Readers.

Armstrong, M. (1982). The story of five stories: an enquiry into children's narrative thought. Unpublished mimeo.

Becker, H. (1958). 'Problems of inference and proof in participant observation'. *American Sociological Review*. Vol. 28, December, p. 652–660 (reprinted in McCormick, op. cit.).

Bolster, A. (1983). 'Towards a more effective model of research on teaching'. *Harvard Educational Review*, Vol. 53, No. 3, p. 294–308.

Bowen, B., Forsyth, K., Green, J., Hurlin, T., Pols, R., Walton, F., and Wood, J. (no date). *Ways of Doing Research on One's Own Classroom*. Cambridge Institute of Education, Ford Teaching Project.

Campbell, D. and Stanley, J. (1963). Experimental and quasi-experimental designs for research on teaching. In Gage, N. (ed.). *Handbook of Research on Teaching*. Chicago, Rand McNally.

Carr, W. and Kemmis, S. (1983). *Becoming Critical: Knowing Through Action Research*. Victoria, Deakin University Press.

Chanan, G. and Delamont, S. (eds.) (1975). *Frontiers of Classroom Research*. Windsor, NFER.

Cogan, M. (1973). *Clinical Supervision*. Boston, Houghton Mifflin.

Congdon, P. (1978). 'Basic Principles of Sociometry'. *Association of Educational Psychologists Journal*, Vol. 4, No. 8, p. 5–9.

Cronbach, L. (1975), 'Beyond the two disciplines of scientific psychology'. *American Psychologist*, Vol. 30, No. 2, p. 116–127.

Dillon, J. (1983). 'Problem Solving and Findings'. *The Journal of Creative Behaviour*, Vol. 16, No. 2 Second Quarter, p. 97–111.

Dunn, W. and Swierczek, F. (1977). 'Planned organizational change: toward grounded theory'. *Journal of Applied Behavioural Science*, Vol. 13, No. 2, p. 135–157.

Ebbutt, D. (1983). Educational action research: some general concerns and specific quibbles. Cambridge Institute of Education, mimeo.

Ebbutt, D. and Elliott, J. (eds.) (1985). *Issues in Teaching for Understanding*. York, Longman.

Elbaz, F. (1983). *Teacher Thinking – a Study of Practical Knowledge.* London, Croom Helm.

Elliott, J. (1976). *Developing Hypotheses about Classrooms from Teachers Practical Constructs.* Cambridge, Ford Teaching Project.

Elliott, J. (1981). Action research: framework for self-evaluation in schools. TIQL working paper no. 1. Cambridge Institute of Education, mimeo.

Elliott, J. and Adelman, C. (1976). *Innovation at the classroom level: A case study of the Ford Teaching Project.* Unit 28, Open University Course E 203: Curriculum Design & Development. Milton Keynes, Open University Press.

Elliott, J. and Ebbutt, D. (1985a). *Facilitating Educational Action Research in Schools.* York, Longman.

Elliott, J. and Ebbutt, D. (eds.) (1985b). *Case Studies in Teaching for Understanding.* Cambridge, Cambridge Institute of Education.

Fisher, R. (1935). *The Design of Experiments.* Edinburgh, Oliver & Boyd.

Flanders, N. (1970). *Analysing Teaching Behaviour.* Reading, Mass., Addison-Wesley.

Freire, P. (1972). *Pedagogy of the Oppressed.* Hamondsworth, Penguin.

Gage, N. (1978). *The Scientific Basis of the Art of Teaching.* New York, Teachers College Press.

Galton, M. (1978). *British Mirrors.* Leicester, University of Leicester School of Education.

Gambrell, L. (1981). 'Extending think-time for better reading instruction'. *Education Digest,* February, p. 33–35.

Glaser, B. & Strauss, A. (1967). *The Discovery of Grounded Theory.* New York, Aldine.

Goldhammer, R., Anderson, R., Krajewski, R. (1980). *Clinical Supervision: Special Methods for the Supervision of Teachers.* (2nd Edition) New York, Holt, Rinehart and Winston.

Good, T. and Brophy, J. (1978) *Looking in Classrooms.* (2nd Edition) New York, Harper & Row.

Guba, E. (1978). *Towards a Methodology of Naturalistic Inquiry in Educational Evaluation.* Los Angeles, Centre for the Study of Evaluation, UCLA.

Hamilton, D., Macdonald, B., King, C., Jenkins, D., Parlett, M. (eds). (1977). *Beyond the Numbers Game.* Berkeley, McCutchan.

Hammersley, M. and Atkinson, P. (1983). *Ethnography: Principles in Practice.* London, Tavistock Publications.

Hopkins, D. (1982). 'Doing research in your own classroom'. *Phi Delta Kappan,* Vol. 64, No. 4, December, p. 274–275.

Hopkins, D. (1984a). 'Teacher research: back to the basics'. *Classroom Action Research Network Bulletin* No. 6, p. 94–99.

Hopkins, D. (1984b). 'Towards a methdology for teacher based classroom research'. *School Organization* Vol 4, No. 3, p. 197–204.

Hopkins, D. (1985). *School Based Review for School Improvement.* Leuven, Belgium, ACCO.

Hopkins, D. and Wideen, M. (1984). *Alternative Perspectives on School Improvement*. Lewes, Falmer.

Hull, C., Rudduck, J. and Sigsworth, A. (1985). *A Room Full of Children Thinking*. York, Longman.

Joyce, B. and Weil, M. (1980). *Models of Teaching*. (2nd Edition) Englewood Cliffs, Prentice Hall.

Joyce, B., Brown, C. and Peck, L. (1981). *Flexibility in Teaching*. New York, Longman.

Joyce, B., Hersh, R. and McKibbin, M. (1983). *The Structure of School Improvement*. New York, Longman.

Joyce, B. and Showers, B. (1980). 'Improving inservice training: the messages of research'. *Educational Leadership*, Vol. 37, No. 5, February, p. 379–385.

Joyce, B. and Showers, B. (1984). 'Transfer of Training: the Contribution of Coaching'. In Hopkins and Wideen, op. cit..

Kemmis, S. (1983). 'Action Research'. In Husen, T. and Postlethwaite, T. (eds.). *International Encyclopedia of Education: Research and Studies*. Oxford, Pergamon.

Kemmis, S. and McTaggart, R. (1981). *The Action Research Planner*. Victoria, Australia, Deakin University Press.

Lewin, K. (1946). 'Action research and minority problems'. *Journal of Social Issues*, vol. 2. p. 34–46.

Lortie, D. (1975). *School Teacher*. Chicago, University of Chicago Press.

MacDonald, B. and Walker R. (eds.) (1974). *Innovation, Evaluation Research and the Problem of Control*. Norwich, C.A.R.E., University of East Anglia Press.

Magee, B. (1973). *Popper*. London, Fontana/Collins.

May, N. and Rudduck, J. (1983). *Sex Stereotyping and the Early Years of Schooling*. Norwich, School of Education, University of East Anglia Press.

McCormick, R. (ed.) (1982). *Calling Education to Account*. London, Heinemann.

McKibbin, M. and Joyce, B. (1980). 'Psychological States and Staff Development' *Theory into Practice*, Vol. XIX, No. 4, Autumn, p. 248–255.

McMahon, A., Bolam, R., Abbott, R. and Holly, P. (1984). *Guidelines for Review and Internal Development in Schools*, York, Longman.

Nixon, J. (ed.) (1981). *A Teacher's Guide to Action Research*. London, Grant and McIntyre.

Nuttall, D. (1981). *School Self Evaluation: Accountability with a Human Face*. York, Longman.

Open University. (1976). *Personality and Learning*. Course E 201, Block II, Milton Keynes, Open University Press.

Polyani, M. (1962). *Personal Knowledge*. Chicago, University of Chicago Press.

Pring, R. (1978). Teacher as Researcher. In Lawton, D. *et al. Theory and Practice of Curriculum Studies*. London, Routledge and Kegan Paul.

Rapoport, R. (1970). 'Three Dilemmas in Action Research'. *Human Relations*, Vol. 23, p. 1–11.

Rowland, S. (1984). *The Enquiring Classroom: an Introduction to Childrens Learning*. Lewes, Falmer.

Rudduck, J. (ed.) (1982). *Teachers in Partnership: Four Studies of Inservice Collaboration*. York, Longman.

Rudduck, J. (1981). *Making the most of the Short Inservice Course*. London, Methuen.

Rudduck, J. (1984). Introducing Innovation to Pupils. In Hopkins and Wideen, op. cit..

Rudduck, J. and Hopkins, D. (eds.) (1985). *Research as a Basis for Teaching*. London, Heinemann.

Sandford, N. (1970). 'Whatever happened to action research?' *Journal of Social Issues*, p. 3–23.

Schon, D. (1983). *The Reflective Practitioner*. New York, Basic Books.

Simon, A. and Boyer, E. (1975). *Mirrors for Behaviour: an Anthology of Classroom Observation Instruments*. Philadelphia, Research for Better Schools Inc..

Simons, H. (ed.) (1980). *Towards a Science of the Singular*. Norwich, C.A.R.E., University of East Anglia Press.

Simons, H. (1982). Suggestions for a school self evaluation based on democratic principles. In McCormick, op. cit..

Smith, L. and Geoffrey, W. (1968). *The Complexities of an Urban Classroom*. New York, Holt, Rinehart and Wilson.

Sockett, H. (ed.). (1980). *Accountability in the English Educational System*. London, Hodder and Stoughton.

Stenhouse, L. (1970). *The Humanities Project*. London: Heinemann, (anonymously), revised edition by Rudduck, J. (1983). Norwich, School of Education, University of East Anglia Press.

Stenhouse, L. (1975). *An Introduction to Curriculum Research and Development*. London, Heinemann.

Stenhouse, L. (1979). Using Research means doing research. In Dahl, H. *et al*. (eds). *Spotlight on Educational Research*. Oslo, University Press.

Stenhouse, L. (1980). 'Product or process: a response to Brian Crittenden'. *New Education*, Vol. 2, No. 1, p. 137–140.

Stenhouse, L. (1983). *Authority, Education and Emancipation*. London, Heinemann.

Stenhouse, L. (1984). Artistry and teaching: the teacher as focus of research and development. In Hopkins and Wideen, op. cit..

Stenhouse, L., Verma, G., Wild, R., and Nixon, J. (1982). *Teaching About Race Relations*. London, Routledge and Kegan Paul.

Walker, R. and Adelman, C. (1975). *A Guide to Classroom Observation*. London, Methuen.

Whitman, W. (1959). *Leaves of Grass*. New York, Viking. (First edition 1855).

Appendix A: Classroom Action Research Network

The Classroom Action Research Network (CARN) which incorporates the Ford Teaching Project provides a well organized network for teacher–researchers. CARN publishes all the Ford Teaching Project books and materials, and organizes conferences at which teacher–researchers are encouraged to discuss and make presentations on their work. Published annually is the *CARN Bulletin* that contains papers, bibliographies, a membership list and details of services offered by members. CARN's membership is broad and eclectic, and membership of the network is invaluable for any aspiring or practising teacher–researcher. For further information contact:

CLASSROOM ACTION RESEARCH NETWORK,
CAMBRIDGE INSTITUTE OF EDUCATION,
SHAFTESBURY ROAD,
CAMBRIDGE, CB2 2BX,
ENGLAND U.K.
Telephone Cambridge (0223) 69631.

Appendix B: Ethics for Classroom Research

Action researchers must pay attention to the ethical principles guiding their work. Their actions are deeply embedded in an existing social organization and the failure to work within the general procedures of that organization may not only jeopardise the process of improvement but existing valuable work. Principles of procedure for action research accordingly go beyond the usual concerns for confidentiality and respect for the persons who are the subjects of enquiry and define in addition, appropriate ways of working with other participants in the social organization. The principles outlined below reflect the commitment implicit in the methods of action research to participation and collaborative work, and negotiation within, and ultimately beyond existing social and political circumstances.

Observe protocol: Take care to ensure that the relevant persons, committees and authorities have been consulted, informed and that the necessary permission and approval has been obtained.

Involve participants: Encourage others who have a stake in the improvement you envisage to shape the form of the work

Negotiate with those affected: Not everyone will want to be directly involved; your work should take account of the responsibilities and wishes of others

Report progress: Keep the work visible and remain open to suggestions so that unforeseen and unseen ramifications can be taken account of; colleagues must have the opportunity to lodge a protest to you

Obtain explicit authorization before you observe: For the purposes of recording the activities of professional colleagues or others (the observation of your own students falls outside this imperative provided that your aim is the improvement of teaching and learning)

Obtain explicit authorization before you examine files, correspondence or other documentation: Take copies only if specific authority to do this is obtained

Negotiate descriptions of people's work: Always allow those described to challenge your accounts on the grounds of fairness, relevance and accuracy

Negotiate accounts of others' points of view (e.g., in accounts of communication): Always allow those involved in interviews, meetings and written exchanges to require amendments which enhance fairness, relevance and accuracy

Obtain explicit authorization before using quotations: Verbatim transcripts, attributed observations, excerpts of audio and video recordings, judgements, conclusions or recommendations in reports (written or to meetings)

Negotiate reports for various levels of release: Remember that different audiences demand different kinds of reports; what is appropriate for an informal verbal report to a faculty meeting may not be appropriate for a staff meeting, a report to council, a journal article, a newspaper, a newsletter to parents; be conservative if you cannot control distribution.

Accept responsibility for maintaining confidentiality

Retain the right to report your work: Provided that those involved are satisfied with the fairness, accuracy and relevance of accounts which pertain to them; and that the accounts do not unnecessarily expose or embarrass those involved; then accounts should not be subject to veto or be sheltered by prohibitions of confidentiality

Make your principles of procedure binding and known: All of the people involved in your action research project must agree to the principles before the work begins; others must be aware of their rights in the process

Reprinted, with permission, from the *Action Research Planner* (Kemmis and McTaggart, 1981: 43–44).

Subject Index

Name Index